What people are saying about Jane Boucher and her book...

"This book is a powerful tool that can change women's lives."

—*Valerie K. Sorosiak*
Professional clinical counselor

"I feel grateful for Jane Boucher's book and for all the other women who have broken the silence and created visible strategies that have empowered women."

—*Olympia Dukakis*
Academy Award-winning actor

"If you are in an abusive relationship, please read this book."

—*Diana Curran, M.D.*
Assistant Professor, Department of Obstetrics and Gynecology, University of Michigan Health System Ann Arbor, Michigan

"Jane Boucher's book is enlightening and inspiring for all who seek freedom from oppressive relationships. *Escaping Domestic Abuse* breaks new ground and doesn't look back."

—*Patricia Evans*
Pioneer researcher of domestic violence issues
Best-selling author of The Verbally Abusive Relationship

"In my thirty years as a lawyer and judge, Jane's book is the best I have ever seen to provide help in a way we have never had before. This work will save lives!"

—*Honorable Stephen Wolaver*
Judge, Greene County, Ohio

"A book like this is desperately needed to give women the know-how and the courage to do what is best for their lives."

—Tony Campolo
Professor Emeritus, Eastern University,
St. David's, Pennsylvania
Spiritual adviser to United States presidents
Respected lecturer on family values

"It's a myth to assume that domestic violence victims invite abuse if they stay in an abusive relationship. Being abused slowly changes the brain's chemistry. Jane's book dispels that myth."

—Christina O'Neil
Miss Nevada 2003

"Women must break their silence and come together as a group to end this age-old dilemma. Jane's book helps break the silence."

—Jackie Kallen
Noted female boxing manager whose life was portrayed
by Meg Ryan in the movie Against the Ropes

"*Escaping Domestic Abuse* is a much needed escape plan for women experiencing relationship violence."

—Walt Dimitroff
Nevada marriage and family therapist

Escaping
DOMESTIC ABUSE

Escaping
DOMESTIC ABUSE

How Women Get Out and Stay Out

JANE BOUCHER

WHITAKER
HOUSE

ESCAPING DOMESTIC ABUSE

How Women Get Out and Stay Out

Jane Boucher
jane@janeboucher.com
janeboucher.com

ISBN: 978-1-60374-091-3
Printed in the United States of America
© 2009 by Jane Boucher

Whitaker House
1030 Hunt Valley Circle
New Kensington, PA 15068
www.whitakerhouse.com

Library of Congress Cataloging-in-Publication Data

Boucher, Jane.
   Escaping domestic abuse / by Jane Boucher.
      p. cm.
   Includes bibliographical references.
   Summary: "Statistical data, expert testimony, and personal stories of survival equip readers to recognize and escape—or help others escape—from abusive relationships and discover a life of freedom from fear and torment"—Provided by publisher.
   ISBN 978-1-60374-091-3 (trade pbk. : alk. paper) 1. Abused women. 2. Family violence. I. Title.
   HV6626.B677 2009
   362.82'92—dc22
                              2008052091

1 2 3 4 5 6 7 8 9 10 11 12   ᴜᴊ   16 15 14 13 12 11 10 09

*For Sarah
and all the other children who never
had the chance to grow up.*

ACKNOWLEDGMENTS

I am so grateful for the people who took the time to voice their support of this book: Dawn Gibbons, Olympia Dukakis, Patricia Evans, Honorable Stephen Wolaver, Tony Campolo, Christina O'Neil, Jackie Kallen, Walt Dimitroff, Valerie Sorosiak, Diana Curran, M.D., and Honorable Scott Jordan.

I dedicate this book to Dr. Matia Brizman, whose brilliance and care made this book a reality.

I am eternally grateful to my VPOE (Vice President of Everything), Bobbie Puterbaugh, who is my daily conscience and right hand.

Thank you, Marlene Brandon, my friend and my sister, for your unfailing love and constant support.

My sincere gratitude goes to Christine Whitaker and the entire Whitaker House team, who believed in my idea and caught the vision, and to my editor, Courtney Hartzel, for making this a masterpiece.

Thank you, Denesa Johnston, whose constant encouragement, friendship, and sisterhood have made this book a reality.

Last, but certainly not least, I want to thank Betty Kossick. She was one of my first students, and she graciously offered to interview many of the survivors whose stories are told in this book.

To protect your confidentiality, I am withholding names. You know who you are. Many of you had the courage to open old wounds. You shared your secrets and your success stories. I sincerely thank you for contributing to this very important book, one that I hope is comprehensive enough to be the only tool people will ever need to get out and stay out of an abusive relationship. Ralph Waldo Emerson, U.S. essayist and poet, said it well: "To leave the world a bit better, whether by a healthy child, a garden patch or a redeemed social condition; to know even one life has breathed easier because you have lived. This is to have succeeded."

Thank you for caring.

CONTENTS

FOREWORD

It is an honor to write the foreword to this very important book. Domestic abuse is present in all levels of society. To ignore it is to permit it to continue. As a practicing obstetrician-gynecologist for more than twelve years, I have witnessed many women suffering from emotional, physical, and sexual abuse. Although my experience is with women, men are abused, as well. The overwhelming majority of abuse occurs against women. Abuse of women has far-reaching health consequences for a woman and her children.

Women who have been in abusive relationships suffer higher rates of health problems and social dysfunction. Many women are unable to obtain psychiatric care due to a lack of resources, an unawareness of mental health services, and a fear of the stigma of depression. Women who have suffered abuse are less productive at work, and millions of dollars are lost each year due to domestic violence. Other consequences include social isolation due to lost relationships.

Many women stay in abusive relationships because they have children. Often, women stay because of an inability to support themselves and their children. Fifty percent of children in houses where one parent is abused are abused themselves by a parent or the partner. Finding the courage to break free from the tangled bonds an abuser weaves takes strength and determination. Escaping is often scary, but the long-term benefits for women and their children are priceless.

If you are in an abusive relationship, please read this book and take heart. The courageous stories in Jane Boucher's book serve as beacons of hope. This book is a guide for abused women and for those who care about them. Thank you, Jane.

—Diana Curran, M.D.
Assistant Professor, Department of Obstetrics and Gynecology
University of Michigan Health System
Ann Arbor, Michigan

PREFACE

This book will be especially helpful to:

    1) You who are being abused by a spouse or intimate partner.

2) You who have made the decision to leave and sincerely want to stay away.

3) Anyone who has been touched by domestic violence in any way. You may be part of a victim's support system. This book will keep you from giving up on her.

4) The employers of victims. Domestic violence doesn't stay home when its victims go to work. Often, the offender follows, resulting in violence in the workplace. In addition, domestic violence usually causes decreased productivity and increased absence due to illness or injury.

We need to stop minding our own business. What do I mean by that? Recently, one of my adult students called to share a story with me. She wanted to know whether she had done the wrong thing. She had been driving behind a car in which a man was slugging the woman next to him. My student did not dial 9-1-1, even though she could see the license plate number. She said the woman looked passive; her demeanor seemed to indicate that getting slugged was "normal" to her. *Escaping Domestic Abuse: How Women Get Out and Stay Out*

15

> ೧
>
> Many women suffer in silence because of the shame that is usually attached to domestic violence.

will tell you why the woman in the car showed little resistance to her violent male companion. She had become numb to the abuse.

Once, when I was traveling by plane, I noticed that one of the flight attendants wore on her lapel a pin depicting two silver hands touching. Intrigued, I started a discussion with the woman, whose name is Renee Jepsen. She told me that she had learned sign language and was working with Dove, a service that advocates on behalf of deaf women and children who have been victims of abuse. Many hearing women suffer in silence because of the shame that is usually attached to domestic violence. Imagine the added silence—and suffering—as a result of deafness. One deaf woman was arrested because her abuser spoke for her. The police officer did not understand sign language and could not interpret her body language, so he assumed she was guilty. A deaf mother may be afraid to leave her abuser for fear that her children will be taken away from her. After all, the court may decide, often based on the abuser's persuasion, that a deaf mother cannot care for her child adequately if she cannot hear it cry, for example.

Many brave people have come together and shared their stories to help make *Escaping Domestic Abuse: How Women Get Out and Stay Out* a powerful survival manual. They have given voices to those who suffer in silence. The primary purpose of this book is to teach the reader how to stop the revolving door of abuse or to help someone else escape an abusive relationship. Most victims return to their abuser eight to eleven times before they finally get out for good. Those of you who had the bravery to share your stories are heroes, indeed.

I am ashamed to admit that until September 11, 2001, I did not know about the plight of Afghan women. Similarly, I believe that most Americans do not know that abuse exists in every neighborhood and has nothing to do with socioeconomic status or educational level. Yes, it is an unpleasant topic. Most of us would prefer blissful ignorance. We don't want to admit that abuse exists in our families, our neighborhoods, our churches, and, God forbid, in our own marriages. We think that if we don't address it, it must not exist. The fact remains that one out of three families experiences the terror of abuse inside the home. Yours may be one of them. In this book are the tools to help you get out—and to stay out once you've gotten out. Put this book in a safe, private place. If you are able to admit and accept that abuse is happening to you or someone you know, this book is for you. Read it and build the courage to change your life. I'm already proud of you for reading these pages.

I have learned not to give flippant answers to people who are thinking about leaving an abuser. Someone who does not understand the deliberation involved will impatiently exclaim, "Just get out!" "I can't understand why you stay!" "I give up!" or "You must be a masochist." The truth is that most women have good basic instincts. Their reasons for staying with an abuser are usually rational and realistic, as we will discuss further in this book.

What can we do to help? We can stop minding our own business and start realizing that domestic violence is everyone's business. As a first step, we must decide that domestic violence is never acceptable. Abuse is abhorrent to most of us, but if we react with apathy and fail to offer help when we see a woman being beaten in the car in front of us, we simply perpetuate the problem.

This book is unique in that it shows victims of abuse not only how to *get out*, but also how to *stop returning to the abuser.* I hope that the words in this book may save your life or the life of someone you know.

The cycle of abuse can be broken. This book is filled with stories of transformations—stories that have happy endings. You will learn practical steps to take in order to *get out and stay out*, and you will learn how to get your life back. You will read stories of others' struggles and the abuse they endured. But, most importantly, you will hear how they escaped. Each happy ending is actually a beginning of a new, meaningful life.

This book will show you the seven secrets of how to *stay out once you get out* of a destructive relationship. *Escaping Domestic Abuse* begins with real stories about real people. Some of them are uplifting—others are devastating. If you want to go straight for the answers on how to *stay out once you get out*, skip the stories and read chapter 9, which reveals "The Seven Secrets of Staying Out."

You will discover that you are not alone, especially if you have returned numerous times to your abuser. Most women do this many times before finally leaving. Again, you will also learn that it takes time to recover—approximately three months for every year you spent with an abusive partner. Domestic violence is not just a family matter; it is a serious crime that deserves to be treated seriously by friends, family, and employers.

> ℘
> You are not alone, especially if you have returned numerous times to your abuser.

Whether you are trying to manage your own relationship, having recently mustered the courage to leave your abuser, or are being counseled or working with other hurting women, this book will equip you to *get out and stay out once you get out* when getting out is the only option. Even after you say that you've left for good, you may still experience overwhelming urges to return. This book will help you put up barriers to keep you out forever!

In spite of all the physical and emotional turmoil you may have endured, you can create a new life. I want to help you. Your journey to freedom is about to begin. In fact, it is already underway—it began when you picked up this book. With adequate resources and support, you can *begin again*. This book will equip you with the tools needed to *get out and stay out*. I am proud of you for having the courage to decide to change your life, just as I am proud of the many individuals I interviewed for this book who changed their lives by escaping abusive relationships. I have tried to provide true-to-life snapshots of what they went through. Most of their names have been changed to guard their privacy. None of their stories is pretty. All of their situations were tough. If you see yourself in any of these scenarios and you respond by *getting out and staying out*, this book will not have been written in vain.

—Jane Boucher

INTRODUCTION
THE STAGGERING SCOPE AND INSIDIOUS CYCLE OF DOMESTIC ABUSE

Laura and her husband lived with their young daughter, Sarah, in Orlando, Florida. When Laura's husband verbally abused her and then started using physical violence, she sought help from a domestic violence counselor. She learned that her husband was trying to wield power over her with his escalating abuse, and her eyes were opened to the reality of her situation. When she asked him to leave, he filed for divorce, and their settlement entitled him to weekend visitation with their daughter, Sarah. On November 7, 1996, Sarah was not dropped off at her daycare center. November 7 seemed just like any other day—that is, until Laura's husband's employer called inquiring about his absence at work. Laura's mind started racing. Sure that her ex-husband had kidnapped Sarah, she called 9-1-1. The Orlando police came to Laura's workplace, and she drove with them to her husband's apartment. When they arrived, the area was cordoned off. Laura's eyes met those of a victim's advocate, and she knew the worst had happened. Still, Laura asked, "Is Sarah okay?" When the advocate looked away, Laura asked, "Is she dead?" The advocate nodded. Sarah's father had fired four .45-caliber bullets into Sarah's chest before taking his own life.

Domestic violence is a bigger problem than you might think. One out of every four women in this country will experience domestic violence in her lifetime.[1] But few people know the scope of this

---

[1] Patricia Tjaden and Nancy Thoennes (National Institute of Justice and the Centers of Disease Control and Prevention), "Extent, Nature and Consequences of Intimate Partner Violence: Findings from the National Violence against Women Survey," 2000.

national epidemic, much less understand the nature of how it begins and becomes inescapable. The problem was long swept under the carpet by cultural norms and gender traditions that treated what we classify as "abuse" as a nonissue. In the 1920s, social workers considered battered women to be mentally retarded. In the 1940s, psychologists claimed that battered women were masochistic; in other words, women who were battered *liked* being abused. In the State of Arkansas, an archaic law that legalizes beating one's wife once a month remains on the books, and the phrase "rule of thumb" originally meant that it was acceptable for a husband to beat his wife with a stick as long as it was no wider than his thumb.

People are finally waking up to the gravity of this problem in our country and around the world, but misconceptions still abound, and counselors, psychologists, and other professionals aren't immune to this ignorance, either. Many of the people I interviewed in writing this book had taken their abusive spouses to meet with counselors who came highly recommended. One particular story is of a woman who took her husband to meet with a therapist, only to be attacked verbally by the counselor during their second session. The counselor exploded, "If you'd only go to Al-Anon! Why haven't you gone yet? You have no one to blame but yourself for all of these marital problems!" The therapist whose help this woman was seeking to keep her marriage together actually told her that if she would learn to detach, all would be well. The woman responded, "I did not get married to detach."

> ❧
>
> Domestic violence experts know that being "more unconditionally loving" will never solve the problem.

On top of this confusion, many therapists who don't know any better tell victims of domestic abuse simply to "love him harder" or "love him more unconditionally." They remind them, "It always takes two." But nothing could be further from the truth. Domestic violence experts know that being "more unconditionally loving" will never solve the problem, and that in abusive relationships, "it does not take two; it only takes one." In fact, overlooking the abusive behavior and loving someone in spite of it often makes the abuse worse.

Many women stay with their abusive partners or spouses because of the fear of retribution—if they leave, they know they may be harmed or killed. Lisa Bianco's husband was in prison for assaulting her and kidnapping their children. His good behavior earned him a day pass, and on his day away from prison, he drove to Lisa's Indiana home and clubbed her to death. Lisa's grieving mother told television reporters, "People ask, 'Why don't battered women leave?' They get killed...."

Starting over isn't easy. Leaving an abuser for good can be an extremely difficult decision to make. I hope that this book will help you feel less alone. Current research helps explain why people stay with their abusers. Now, you can learn how to stay *away*. You can also learn that there is life after abuse.

Why do you stay? The reasons are highly complex, and they vary from woman to woman. You may be lonely, depressed, or in poor health; you may lack self-esteem or self-confidence. Maybe you're afraid of further abuse or violence; you may fear taking the risk of leaving. Perhaps you feel guilty. Perhaps you have no place to go, no family to take you in, and no access to money. Maybe your religious beliefs or ethnic traditions compel you to stay...the list goes on. You need to be understood and *not judged* for deciding to stay for however long you may have remained with your abuser. Unfortunately, even our legal and social systems will often give up on you if you return again and again to the abusive relationship. With courage and wise counsel, you can break the cycle. The good news is that most women eventually leave their abusers for good. You need to understand that leaving is a process, not an event!

Add to this scenario the fact that most women living in abusive home environments become physically ill. Many gynecological, urinary, and bowel problems can result from constant emotional abuse, and in 2000, a study coauthored by Dr. Brenda B. Toner linked women's experience of emotional abuse with irritable bowel syndrome (IBS), a digestive disorder.[2] Worse, this long-term stress can cause heart disease, chronic pain, and even cancer. There is a direct correlation between abuse and disease. If you have an abuse-related illness or disease, your life is often out of balance and out of "ease." The distress in your life will cause dis-ease, which means your life is out of ease. *Your body knows what your mind cannot accept.* Your relationship is toxic. As the years pass and the abuse escalates, your body responds in kind. Listen to your body. It is screaming for you to relax. Your body is a gifted communicator. It may motivate you to leave. You will not get well as long as you remain in a sick relationship. On the other hand, if you leave and find peace elsewhere, your body will respond positively. You will get well again.

Research shows that most batterers are men. In 2001, 85 percent of the victims of intimate partner violence were women, totaling 588,490.[3] But it is quite possible for a female to abuse a male partner, so if you are a man being battered, simply change the feminine pronouns to masculine ones throughout this book. It is important to understand that this book was not written to hurt or indict "him." If, by helping *her*, this book helps *him*, too, that's a bonus. Furthermore, this book is not written to condemn an entire population of men. There are many good men who despise what the abusive man represents and practices.

Domestic violence is *not* caused by alcohol use or drug addictions. People may try to blame domestic violence on substance abuse, but half of all batterers do not use drugs or drink. Abuse does *not* happen because you cooked the wrong meal for dinner or because another man looked at you. It is *not* happening because you spent too long at the grocery store. It is *not* happening because your abuser just

---

[2] Alisha Ali, Brenda B. Toner, Noreen Stuckless, Ruth Gallop, Nicholas E. Diamant, Michael I. Gould, and Eva I. Vidins, "Emotional Abuse, Self-Blame, and Self-Silencing in Women with Irritable Bowel Syndrome," *Psychosomatic Medicine* 62 [Issue 1] (January/February 2000): 76–82.

[3] Bureau of Justice Statistics Crime Data Brief, Intimate Partner Violence, 1993–2001, February 2003.

"snapped" or is "out of control." Just the opposite. Abuse is all about *power and control*. The abuser's behavior is quite intentional, and you are not to blame.

Maybe you have already escaped an abuser and are now encountering the daily challenges of your new life of freedom. Within the first five minutes of this newfound freedom, some of you will have these internal conversations: *Why did he treat me the way he did? Why did I lose my life, my career, my friends, my family—even my church—why didn't people believe me? He treated me so lovingly in public, but no one saw how he was in private. And why do I still vacillate in my feelings toward him? Why does he get to keep his career, his life, our family, and our church?*

> ✃
>
> The abuser's behavior is quite intentional, and you are not to blame.

It takes many women an experience near death in order to wake up. Some of you never suffered physical harm, but your spirits were broken. You may have lost your identity to an abuser who snuffed it out or stole it away. You became accustomed to something that should never be normal or customary. It often takes many years to reclaim your broken pieces. It takes approximately three months for every year you remained with an abuser to recover fully once you've escaped.

On a global level, one out of three women is abused, according to a United Nations report released on October 10, 2006.[4] The United States Department of Justice reports that women are the primary victims of intimate partner violence.[5] The majority of domestic violence occurrences are those committed by men against a female partner, but abuse of a male partner is a troubling but little discussed issue. *In fact, a leading cause of death among pregnant women is*

---

[4] "Violence against Women: Causes and Costs of a Global Curse," *DESA News* 10, no. 6 (November–December 2006): 1–4.

[5] *Injury Research Agenda.* Centers for Disease Control and Prevention, 2006.

murder.[6] *And usually at the hand of a husband or intimate partner.*[7] The statistics below will help you to gain a better understanding of the scope of domestic violence, both in this country and in the world.

The Staggering Scope of Domestic Violence

- Every fifteen seconds, a woman somewhere in America is battered, usually by her husband or intimate partner.[8]

- Every day, 1,871 women in the U.S. are raped.[9]

- One-third of all murdered women are killed by their husbands or boyfriends.[10]

- Every day in our country, more than three women are murdered by a husband or intimate partner.[11]

- One-third of American women will experience intimate partner violence at some point in their lives.[12]

- According to the National Coalition against Domestic Violence, a woman is battered by her husband or boyfriend in this country every fifteen seconds, which makes domestic violence the most common crime—and least reported one—in the U.S.

---

[6] Jeani Chang, Cynthia J. Berg, Linda E. Saltzman, and Joy Herndon, *Homicide: A Leading Cause of Injury Deaths among Pregnant and Postpartum Women in the United States, 1991–1999.* Centers for Disease Control and Prevention: *American Journal of Public Health* 25, no. 3 (March 2005): 471–477.

[7] Victoria Frye, "Examining Homicide's Contribution to Pregnancy-Associated Deaths," *The Journal of the American Medical Association* 285, no. 11 (2001): 1510–1511.

[8] *UN Study on the Status of Women, 2000.*

[9] National Victim Center and Crime Victims Research and Treatment Center, 1992.

[10] Federal Bureau of Investigation, *Uniform Crime Reports,* "Crime in the United States, 2000," 2001.

[11] Bureau of Justice Statistics Crime Data Brief, *Intimate Partner Violence, 1993–2001,* February 2003.

[12] The Commonwealth Fund, "Health Concerns Across a Woman's Lifespan: The Commonwealth Fund 1998 Survey of Women's Health," May 1989.

- In fact, physical battery is the number one cause of injuries among women—more than automobile accidents, rapes, and muggings combined.[13]

- Princeton Survey Research Associates conducted a two-year study of 3,300 women. The results, released in 2003, revealed that the women's own personal safety was the issue of most concern—of greater concern than even work or other personal priorities.

- Every year, more than one million women seek medical assistance for injuries they incurred as a result of being battered.[14]

- Every year, domestic violence results in almost 100,000 days of hospitalizations, almost 30,000 emergency room visits, and almost 40,000 visits to a physician.[15]

- The Blue Shield Institute says that the total health-care costs of family violence are in the hundreds of millions each year.[16]

- Domestic abuse accounts for three times as many emergency room visits by women as motor vehicle accidents and muggings combined.[17]

- The U.S. Department of Justice estimates that 37 percent of women who end up in the emergency room are there because they were abused by a husband or boyfriend.[18]

---

[13] League of Women Voters of New Jersey Education Fund, 1999–2000.

[14] Evan Stark and Ann Flitcraft, "Medical Therapy as Repression: The Case of the Battered Woman," *Health and Medicine* (Summer/Fall 1981): 29–32.

[15] Ellen W. Ninger, "Addressing the Needs of DV Victims in the Emergency Room," *Coalition Reporter* (New Jersey Coalition for Battered Women) (December 1999): 3–4.

[16] Pennsylvania Blue Shield Institute, *Social Problems and Rising Health Care Costs in Pennsylvania*, 1992: 3–5.

[17] CMA White Paper, "Report on Physicians Confronting Violence in California," August 1995. Copies: CMA FAX ON DEMAND 800/592–4262.

[18] U.S. Department of Justice, *Violence Related Injuries Treated in Hospital Emergency Departments*, August 1997.

- Fifty percent of the men who assault their wives also frequently abuse their children.[19]

- As domestic violence against women becomes more severe and more frequent, children experience a 300 percent increase in physical violence by male batterers.[20]

- Even children whose fathers do not injure them physically still suffer emotional, developmental, and psychological damage.[21]

- Most adult males who are incarcerated were either childhood victims of abuse or witnessed it in their homes.[22]

- If a boy watches his father abuse his mother—or witnesses another type of adult-to-adult violence during his childhood—he is seven hundred times more likely to become an abuser himself and beat his female partner, according to the Sam Houston State University Counseling Center.

- Ninety-four percent of corporate security directors rank domestic violence as a high security problem within their organizations.[23]

- Some people believe that if they are not being physically abused but are "only" emotionally abused, they are not *really* being abused. Nothing could be further from the truth. The threat alone of physical violence or imminent harm is often as

[19] Murray A. Strauss, Richard J. Gelles, and Christine Smith, *Physical Violence in American Families: Risk Factors and Adaptations to Violence in 8,145 Families* (New Brunswick: Transaction Publishers, 1990).

[20] Murray A. Straus and Richard J. Gelles, *Physical Violence in American Families: Risk Factors and Adaptations to Violence in 8,145 Families* (Piscataway, New Jersey: Transaction Publishers, 1999), 386.

[21] S. A. Graham-Bermann and J. Seng, J. "Violence Exposure and Traumatic Stress Symptoms as Additional Predictors of Health Problems in High-Risk Children," *Journal of Pediatrics* 146 [Issue 3] (2005): 309–310.

[22] 2000 Pennsylvania prison study, cited by SAFENET, Erie, Pa.

[23] National Safe Workplace Institute survey, as cited in "Talking Frankly about Domestic Violence," *Personnel Journal*, 1995.

damaging as being physically hurt. (Remember the scene from the film *The Godfather* in which a dead horse's bloody head was placed in the bed? The message was clear.)

- Abuse of any kind can cause long-term anxiety and post-traumatic stress disorder, a psychiatric disorder that can occur following one's experience of a life-threatening event.

- For every year a woman spends with an abusive partner or spouse, three months are required for recovery. In other words, if you were with an abusive partner for ten years, you might need two and a half years to recover.

- One of every five female high school students has been sexually or physically abused by a boyfriend.[24]

- In 1996, a survey conducted for the Advertising Council and the Family Violence Prevention Fund reported that 30 percent of Americans know a woman who has been physically abused by her husband or boyfriend in the past year.[25]

- The United Nations Children's Fund (UNICEF) predicts that between one-quarter and one-half of women worldwide have suffered physical abuse by an intimate partner.[26]

- Every year, an estimated two to four million women of all races and classes are battered by a spouse or intimate partner in the United States (The Family Prevention Fund, San Francisco, California).

- At least 6 percent of pregnant women are battered by their spouses or partners.[27]

---

[24] Jay G. Silverman, Anita Raj, Lorelei A. Mucci, and Jeanne E. Hathaway, "Dating Violence Against Adolescent Girls and Associated Substance Use, Unhealthy Weight Control, Sexual Risk Behavior, Pregnancy, and Suicidality," *Journal of the American Medical Association* 286, no. 5 (2001): 572–579.

[25] Lieberman Research Inc., Tracking Survey conducted for The Advertising Council and the Family Violence Prevention Fund, July–October 1996.

[26] World Health Organization, *Violence against Women*, 1996. WHO Consultation, Geneva: WHO, quoted in "Domestic Violence against Women and Girls," *Innocenti Digest* no. 6 (June 2000): 2.

[27] Centers for Disease Control and Prevention, *The Atlanta Journal and Constitution*, 1994.

- Of all homeless women and children in the U.S., 50 percent are fleeing domestic violence.[28]

- Between 2001 and 2005, more than 80 percent of assaults committed by spouses, ex-spouses, and boyfriends against women were physical attacks. The remaining cases involved the perpetrators' attempting to attack or threatening violence, either verbally or by showing a weapon.[29]

- Over 90 percent of all domestic violence crimes against spouses or ex-spouses are committed by men.[30]

- In 2000, 1,247 women were killed by an intimate partner.[31]

The American woman typically goes back to her abuser up to eleven times. This behavior is difficult for friends, family members, and legal authorities to comprehend. This book explores the main reasons that women go back repetitively and explains how to break away from the revolving door of abuse.

---

[28] Sen. Joseph Biden, U.S. Senate Committee on the Judiciary, "Violence against Women: Victims of the System," 1991.

[29] *Intimate Partner Violence in the U.S.,* Bureau of Justice Statistics, 2007. Dr. Shannan Catalano, BJS statistician.

[30] United States Bureau of Justice Statistics. *Report to the Nation on Crime and Justice* (Darby, Pennsylvania: Diane Publishing, 1988), 33.

[31] Bureau of Justice Statistics Crime Data Brief, *Intimate Partner Violence, 1993–2001*, February 2003.

SELF TESTS

Truths about Abuse

A True-False Test about Abuse

To gauge your knowledge of domestic abuse, answer the following questions. Then, use the self-assessments to find out whether you are a victim who needs to seek help in escaping an abusive relationship.

1) *An abusive person is someone who loses his or her temper too often.*

   False. *Although someone who is abusive may have a hot temper, domestic violence is more than just a passing mood. It is a pattern of behaviors used to control partners or other family members. Many people who abuse others will do so even when they are not angry.*

2) *People who batter their partners always act abusively toward them.*

   False. *Some people who batter their partners tend to become apologetic and more loving after the abuse, often to manipulate the victim into forgiving them or overlooking the abuse. This cycle of mounting tension and violence, followed by what is sometimes called a "honeymoon period," can confuse people who are being abused.*

3) *Abusers may act quite normally in public and at social events.*

   True. *It is possible for someone to act violently at home but show no signs of being an abuser in public.*

4) *Drinking alcohol or using drugs can cause someone to become a batterer.*

False. *Although many abusers are intoxicated when they become violent, alcohol and drugs themselves are not thought to be the causes of abusive behavior. Research also shows that many recovering alcoholics and addicts still tend to be abusive after becoming clean or sober.*

5) *People who hit their partners do so because the partners won't stop talking, yelling, or telling them what to do.*

False. *Abusers hit people because they need to dominate the relationship. The abused person can act demanding or passive—either way, she will still be hit. It is common for people who abuse their partners to blame these partners for their own abusive behavior.*

6) *The person being abused can make the abuse stop.*

False. *The only person who can stop the abuse is the person being abusive. The person being abused can take steps to protect herself or to increase her safety, but she cannot stop the other person from engaging in abusive behavior.*

7) *People learn to become abusive.*

True. *Violence is a behavior learned in abusive families, on the playground at school, from the media, and from many other observed instances of violent social behavior. On a positive note, violent behavior can also be unlearned; people who believe that violence is an acceptable behavior can also learn that it is not acceptable. This shift, however, takes incredible commitment and can be extremely difficult to instill in an abusive person.*

Are You Being Abused?

- Are you cursed, called names, or blamed whenever things go wrong?

- Is the way you spend "free time" limited exclusively to your partner's interests?

- Does your partner have an alcohol or drug dependency?

- Does your partner control all access to money?

- Is it impossible for you to enjoy outside friendships due to your partner's jealousy?

- Does your partner have a Jekyll and Hyde personality?

- Do you "cover" or make excuses for your partner's behavior?

- Do you do more than a fair share of the work, paid or unpaid?

- Are you forced to have sex when you don't want to?

- Do you feel obligated to ask and obtain permission to do things?

- Are you sometimes punished for "misbehaving"?

- During childhood, was your partner or his mother abused?

- Are you the brunt of humiliating jokes?

- Does your partner make a scene if you express a contrary opinion?

- Do you live in fear of your loved one?

If you answered yes to **one or two** of the above questions, take note of trouble areas and work with your partner to improve them.

If you answered yes to **three or four** of the above questions, seriously examine your relationship and seek help from a qualified counselor.

If you answered yes to **five or six** of the above questions, your relationship is breaking down and abuse is the issue. Go to a counselor who understands domestic violence, and go alone! Relationship counseling is not appropriate at this stage.

If you answered yes to **seven or more** of the above questions, you are absolutely being abused and crisis intervention is needed!

Are You Ready to Leave?

- Are you currently in an abusive relationship? How many years have you been in this relationship?

- Have you lost the self-confidence you had at the beginning of this relationship?

- Did your partner promise to change, and are you still waiting for this to happen?

- How many times have you left him and gone back again? What are the reasons that you keep returning to the relationship? What has been the most difficult part of staying away?

- Do you make excuses for your partner's abusive behavior?

- Is the abuse getting worse?

- What are your physical and emotional symptoms?

- If you have children, how is your relationship affecting them? How is it affecting the other areas of your life?

- Do you have a support system that will help you through this transition?

- Do you have a place where you can live when you leave?

- Do you have adequate financial resources to support yourself apart from your partner?

- Do you see no other alternative but to end this relationship?

- Was there some specific incident that made you realize that there was no turning back?

- Are you really ready to leave?

Keep in mind one woman's mantra: "I have a chance for a life if I leave; I die if I stay."

Identifying Your Relationship Preferences

A. List three or four people (not in your immediate family) with whom you have had an important or significant relationship during the past five years.

1.   3.

2.   4.

B. For each individual in the list above, make a list of his or her most salient characteristics. Examples include: affectionate, critical, good listener, kind, demanding, and so forth.

1. _____ _____ _____ _____

2. _____ _____ _____ _____

3. _____ _____ _____ _____

4. _____ _____ _____ _____

C. Circle the characteristics above that are most important to you in someone with whom you would want to have a significant relationship.

D. Look at List A and write the names below of any significant people from your *childhood* who possessed the characteristics you wrote in List B.

1.   3.

2.   4.

E. Return to List C and cross off all the characteristics but the five most important to you. Write those five here.

1.   4.

2.   5.

3.

On the list above, cross off all but the three most important characteristics.

On the list above, cross off all but the single most important characteristic.

Write   that   most   important   characteristic   here:
_____

This is the most important quality you seek in other people.

What Is a Healthy Relationship?

Put a check mark by the statements that apply to you in your current relationship.

____ You feel you are respected as a person.

____ Your physical and emotional needs are met.

____ You like the other person, and you feel liked in return.

____ You are appreciated and not taken for granted.

____ You are not afraid to be yourself.

____ You can communicate effectively with your partner.

____ You can affirm and support one another.

____ Trust, trust, trust is everywhere.

____ There is an atmosphere of humor and play.

____ Responsibilities are shared.

____ Your privacy is respected.

____ You are not constantly fighting for control.

____ You and your partner admit and seek help for any problems you may have.

____ You want to spend time together.

____ Love is a verb, not a noun.

____ You are growing and the relationship is growing.

____ You feel good about yourself and feel free to be yourself.

Part I

WHY WOMEN STAY OR KEEP COMING BACK

1

"I Just Love Him"

 ❧

Mary's Story

Mary was in the hospital to give birth. By her side in the delivery room was her husband, Tom. After giving birth, Mary was on morphine to ease her pain, so she cannot recall what she said while she was recovering. Whatever it was, Tom didn't like it; the next thing she knew, Mary was with a madman. Tom became violent and loud to the point where the night nurse had to order his removal from Mary's room. Her doctor was afraid for her and for the baby, so he kept her in the hospital for an extra week—something that's unheard of in most hospitals, where doctors usually aim to send patients home as soon as possible. Mary's doctor was frightened for her life, and he told her so. Mary was forced to face the truth: riding her husband's roller coaster of abuse and tenderness was killing her.

To excuse his behavior, Tom wrote Mary a letter that went something like this: "I couldn't help myself. Can't you understand how I was treated when I was growing up? My dad pushed, punched, pulled, screamed, and cursed at me. I was blamed for everything that went wrong at home. I was his scapegoat." Tom's father had terrorized him; now, Tom was terrorizing Mary. Still, Mary felt sorry for him. Many women think that they can love their men out of their pain and emotional scars. This almost never works, as Mary found out. She eventually moved to a new state, made new friends, and started a new life. Today, she enjoys a sense of peace and the knowledge that she is no longer dependent on her ex-husband.

Why Do Women Stay?

Why do you stay with your abuser or continue going back to him? In some of the scenarios described in this book, you will probably notice aspects of yourself. One major reason women stay with their abusers or return to them is *emotional hunger*. Emotional hunger is analogous to physical hunger: you may feel as if you're starving when he is no longer in your life. Often, your emotions will drive your behavior. Most abusers act remorseful after episodes of violence. Your abusive partner may make wonderful promises, shower you with expensive gifts, and even beg for forgiveness. If you are a woman of deep faith, you were taught to forgive and to turn the other cheek when hurt or offended, and you will probably feel guilty if you don't forgive him and start again. You *want* to believe that he will change. After all, wasn't he once your knight in shining armor?

Because women tend to internalize their thoughts and emotions, you may even blame yourself for his violent eruptions, saying to yourself, *If I were a better wife, he wouldn't blow up.* You begin to think that you could be—and should be—a better wife. You begin to believe in your own mind what you've heard him say over and over again about your "inadequacies." His truth becomes what you hold true about yourself. You've also built your life around your relationship with him. You want to believe that counseling, substance abuse treatment, or stress reduction will put a stop to his violence. You want to do something—*anything*—to "fix it."

His Excuse Becomes Your Reality

Women often view their boyfriends, partners, and husbands through a filtered lens. No matter how cruelly he acts, you still see a good man underneath it all. You become skilled at ignoring or blocking out violent outbursts—that is, until they start happening frequently.

He repeats statements such as these: "You never listen to me," "You think you're so perfect," "You're too sensitive," "You can't take a joke," "You're pressuring me," and "You're trying to control me." Many women then look at themselves and perform self-evaluations. They wonder, *Did I listen to him? Did I think I was so perfect?* Then, they blame themselves. If you blame yourself, you will do anything to be what he wants you to be. But however hard you try, you never seem to measure up. Still, you keep trying. At first, the verbal abuse is sporadic. If he had a good day at work, he is in a good mood. But if he had a bad day—watch out! He will invent things to be angry about when he gets home. And when he is angry, he is so articulate that you may believe his logic. *The more you believe him, the more you lose yourself.* When you entered into the relationship, you were self-confident. But the longer you stay in the demeaning situation, the shakier your sense of identity becomes. Suddenly, women who were once independent and self-assured don't know who they are.

By nature, women tend to be nurturers. Without realizing it, you become the caretaker of your significant other. You think you are being helpful by paying his bills and covering for him, making excuses for his eccentric behavior and angry outbursts. In reality, though, you are making it worse for him because he is never faced with the painful consequences of his behavior. You have absorbed the pain on his behalf, and he continues along in blissful obliviousness. A well-meaning wife may consult psychiatrists, doctors, counselors, and pastors in her search for answers. You may stay with your abusive husband because a therapist told you that your husband is depressed. You think, *How can I leave a sick person?* After all, most women take their commitments seriously, especially those sealed with marriage vows. To add fuel to the fire, many therapists tell the women they counsel, "All you have to do is love him more unconditionally," or "It always takes two." Women with

> ❧
> Abused
> women often
> believe that
> they are
> part of the
> problem.

a shaky sense of identity stop trusting themselves and adopt their partners' views of reality instead. Adopting a skewed view of reality keeps many women in abusive relationships for years. Abused women often believe that they are part of the problem. Many pastors, knowing a woman is being abused, still recommend that she stay with the abuser, urging self-sacrifice for the sake of the man she loves.

Why Joint Counseling Doesn't Work

The research on couples who attend domestic violence counseling together is not encouraging. Studies show that 50 percent of the men surveyed abused their partners again within six weeks following treatment. Domestic violence is about *power and control*. The abuser must feel *power over* his victim. He achieves the "power over" feeling by a variety of methods, including abuse—whether emotional, verbal, or physical. His victim feels threatened and intimidated by his behavior. If she speaks up during counseling sessions, she is often afraid of the repercussions she will suffer at home afterward. In fact, couples' counseling can sometimes be counterproductive. Not only is the woman often afraid to tell her truth, but she may also gain an ill-founded sense of relief and hope that keeps her in the destructive relationship even longer. Therapists need to work with victims in private sessions—without the abuser's presence—so that these women can extricate themselves from their harmful relationships.

Often, when you are asked why you stayed for so long, you may answer, "I just love him." He has become your sole source of emotional support—but only because he has isolated you from your family and friends. You know that your relationship is unhealthy, but you don't seem to have the emotional reserves of strength and determination necessary to leave. You continually talk to yourself, making mental excuses for his behavior and telling yourself, *He's not that bad.* You have trouble facing the truth of who he really is. In your heart, you know something is wrong, but the experts are telling you not to give up; your mind makes rationalizations and tells you to stay. You can't imagine life without him. He has become your best friend, your only family. The thought of leaving him terrifies you. You weigh your options, trying to determine what would feel worse: staying with him and enduring the abuse or leaving him and possibly leaving your children. For a time, staying wins out.

Sam's Story

Sam adored his wife, Judy; though she often demeaned him verbally, he would quietly accept it without complaint. One afternoon, they were traveling in a taxi with Judy's sister, Janice, when the driver suddenly drove over a bump, jolting the passengers abruptly. Judy erupted at Sam, then jumped out of the taxi at the next traffic light and ran away, leaving Sam and Janice in the cab. Janice asked Sam what had just happened. She couldn't understand why Judy had blown up at him because of the cab driver's poor driving. Sam said little, but what he did say was in defense of his wife's abusive behavior. Janice told Sam that only a man with no self-esteem would take that kind of verbal abuse. When Sam and Janice finally exited the cab, they entered a jewelry store, where Sam decided to purchase a piece of jewelry for his wife. Further befuddled, Janice asked Sam what he was doing. She wondered why he would reward Judy's unacceptable behavior. He responded, "I can't help myself; *I just love her.*" This happened twenty years ago. Sam and Judy are still together today, and Sam still endures her verbal degradation.

The Roller Coaster of Abuse

Life often runs the course of a roller coaster, filled with ups and downs. The ups are moments of decisiveness—*I'm not going to take this abuse anymore.* The downs are the moments when you buy into your abuser's mentality and think, *Maybe I am stupid—I deserve to be treated this way.* You may be called demeaning names: "bitch," "idiot," "stupid," and so forth. You may feel ashamed that you have "taken" the abuse; you may believe that he is right about your "deficiencies." You may have been mocked or been the object of sarcasm. Self-absorbed, narcissistic people who put others down always have excuses for their behavior—it's never their fault and always the fault of others. In spite of the way he treats you, you still love him.

> ᔥ
> Most abused
> women are in
> love with
> a dream
> or illusion.
> Prince
> Charming
> was a passing
> charade.

Studies show that many women think they're crazy because they love the "good part" of their abusive partners. Furthermore, many women hold to the ideal that "love conquers all." Even though you know you married a Jekyll and Hyde personality, you hope that if you stick it out, he will change: mercurial Mr. Hyde will go away forever and leave the kind, endearing Dr. Jekyll in his wake. You remember how chivalrous he was when you first started dating, and you hope and pray that he will be like that again. Most abused women are in love with a dream or an illusion. Prince Charming was a passing charade. He wasn't the real person with whom you now find yourself.

You start blocking out his ugly outbursts and eventually become numb, completely desensitized to his abusive language and behavior. You tell yourself that you aren't really being abused. But you *are* being abused if you're always afraid to express your opinions or feelings because you know that he will retaliate. You *are* being abused if you are kicked, shoved, chased, slapped, punched, thrown around, or hit with objects he throws at you. Forced sex or sexual behavior that makes you afraid or ashamed is another form of abuse—even in the marriage bed.

Verbal abuse can be even more painful than physical abuse. While bruises from physical abuse will heal, verbal abuse can break your spirit irreparably. Your abuser has probably said or done things to keep your family and friends away, which isolates you further. And if he feels he's been crossed in any way, he'll make it even worse for you. Still, you may keep telling yourself, *I've got to forget the past. I'll make it work.* You take a heavy burden on yourself—one that's impossible to bear, especially alone.

If you have been seeing a therapist, you may have been told to do the impossible. Many well-meaning therapists convince their clients that "it always takes two." In the case of domestic violence, it takes only one to destroy or poison a healthy relationship. Unless the violence has stopped completely and the batterer has completed counseling for his harmful habits, couples' counseling might even increase the level of violence. The primary goal of counseling should be to stop the violence, not necessarily to save the marriage.

Actor Olympia Dukakis said, "I feel grateful for all the women who have broken their silence. These women have created visible strategies that empower women. Unless we speak out, more and more women will suffer. When a woman enters a couple's relationship, she expects mutual nurturing and caring. When her partner destroys this bond, it can be devastating. It also impacts her trust and faith in future relationships."

A Life-Saving Resource

Many women have sought answers to their questions from Patricia Evans, author of *The Verbally Abusive Relationship*. From speaking with her or reading her books, these women come to realize that their abusive partners probably aren't going to change. If they desire new circumstances, some of these women will have to move away from their men—sometimes at a significant distance.

Women frequently suffer physical illness as a result of abuse. Ironically, many men responsible for these symptoms will treat their partners better if they are sickly and dependent. This "caring" treatment reinforces the men's perceived *power and control* over the women. If a woman dares to assert her independence, her partner will probably degrade her even more harshly in an attempt to quash this attitude that threatens his control. Patricia Evans encourages women in unhealthy relationships such as these to break away and stay away—for good. Then and only then will these women get their lives back.

Christina's Story

A prevailing fallacy about domestic violence is the assumption that abused women wouldn't stay with their abusers if they weren't receiving some payoff from the abuse. Debunking this fallacy is the mission of Christina O'Neil, a beautiful young woman who was named Miss Nevada 2003. Since then, she has become an advocate for victims of domestic violence. "It's a myth that victims of abuse like being abused if they stay in the relationship," Christina said. "Nothing could be farther from the truth. Being abused slowly changes a person's brain chemistry. It is like boiling a frog. If you put a frog in a pot of boiling water, it will jump out. However, if you put a frog in a pot of cool water and gradually turn up the heat, the frog will eventually boil to death, never realizing what happened."

Christina continued, "If my ex-boyfriend had walked up to me and punched me in the face the first time I met him, I would have called the police. He did not do that. Instead, the abuse came on *gradually* over the five years I was with him. It began with name-calling and then slowly moved to more aggressive verbal abuse. Then, he threw things. Eventually, he threw things at me. The physical abuse followed, and finally, he tried to kill me."

It's not easy for women to tell their stories of abuse, but Christina and the other women who contributed to this book are *brave* women.

Christina said that a counselor's wisdom changed her life. "The counselor told me that when injured troops come home from war, they often receive a Purple Heart for their bravery. If you have survived domestic violence, do not be ashamed. Instead, award yourself a symbolic Purple Heart. You were also injured and had the courage to overcome incredible obstacles."

Delving into the Dynamics of Abusive Relationships

Let's explore the dynamics of abusive relationships and how they function.

First, read the **myths** about abusive relationships, taken from *The Battered Woman* by Dr. Lenore Walker:

- The battered woman syndrome affects only a small percentage of the population.

- Battered women are masochistic.

- Battered women are crazy.

- Middle-class women do not get battered as frequently or as violently as do poorer women.

- Minority women are battered more frequently than Caucasians.

- Lesbians do not abuse their partners.

- Religious beliefs will prevent battering.

- Battered women are uneducated and have few job skills.

- Batterers are violent in all of their relationships.

- Batterers are unsuccessful and lack resources to cope with the world.

- Drinking excessively makes someone become a batterer.

- Batterers are psychopathic personalities.

- Police can protect the battered woman.

- The batterer is not a loving partner.

- A wife batterer always beats his children, too.

- Once a battered woman, always a battered woman.

- Once a batterer, always a batterer.

- Battered women deserve to be beaten.

- Women abused in prostitution are not really battered women.

- Batterers will cease their violence when they get married.

- Children need their father, even if he is violent.

Why Does She Stay?

> ❧
>
> In reality, abused women who remain with their partners do so for complex reasons.

This is the question most often asked about women who remain with their abusive partners. But we should be asking instead, *Why does anybody batter a woman in the first place?* Our society has a prevailing attitude that tends to blame victims for their own suffering. People think, *Victims of abuse must need or like such treatment; otherwise, wouldn't they leave?* The answer isn't that simple. In reality, abused women who remain with their partners do so for complex reasons. Chaer Robert, director of the Denver Commission on Community Relations, offered the following reasons to explain why women stay with their batterers:

- They feel safer with their batterers because they know what they are up to. Often, he is her only psychological support system, having destroyed her other friendships. Others feel uncomfortable around violence and will withdraw from it.

- They are afraid of their abusers. Victims believe that if they leave the relationship, their abusers will act on threats they've made in the past. Batterers often tell their victims they will hurt or kill them or people close to them, report them for welfare fraud, report them to Children Services, call the police on them for domestic violence, or "out" them to their family, friends, or coworkers. The likelihood that an abused woman will be murdered is greatest when she is attempting to report the abuse or to leave the abusive relationship.[32]

- They are severely depressed and thus cannot take action.

- Batterers often do not get serious consequences for their abusive behavior.

- They are afraid that getting the police involved will only make the violence worse. If a batterer is arrested, he is often released from jail within a few hours. He might go after the victim for reporting the abuse. Even if another person reports the abuse or the state charges the batterer, the batterer will blame the victim. Victims know this and will often deny the abuse to avoid repercussions from the abuser.

- They may not know of any community resources for victims, or if the resources exist, they may not be easily accessed or used. Victims may not know their options.

- They may not receive help from the community because their abusers may be rich, well-known, or respected. Abusers are adept at changing their personalities in public to conceal abusive tendencies.

- They are accustomed to focusing on the needs of their abusers and often ignore their own needs. When they reach out for help, professionals often ask them to make quick decisions about their futures. They are often uncomfortable with quick decision-making, as it may trigger further violence.

- They have no financial resources. If they leave their partners and have nowhere else to turn, they face certain homelessness.

- They are afraid that if they report the violence, their batterers will lose their jobs or have their reputations ruined.

---

[32] Angela Browne, *When Battered Women Kill* (New York: Free Press, 1987).

- They feel ashamed and embarrassed about the abuse.

- They believe that outsiders shouldn't be involved in family matters.

- They feel obligated to pretend that nothing is wrong because of their religious convictions or their beliefs about gender roles. Victims may also define their senses of self-worth by their intimate relationships, however abusive.

- They believe that their children will be better-off in a two-parent household. An abusive father will often use his children's well-being as a way to keep his wife from leaving. He might even threaten to take the children away from their mother or to hurt them if she leaves.

- They feel isolated from their family members and friends. This perceived isolation makes it harder for them to leave their abusive partners or spouses. The batterer may be the only person to whom his victim can turn for support. Because abusers feel threatened by the relationships their victims have with other people, they often try to keep them from growing close to others and spending time with friends outside the home.

- They may receive only limited support from family and friends. Victims make an average of four attempts to leave before actually succeeding. People close to the victims may not understand that leaving an abusive relationship is a long and difficult process. They will blame the victims when they return to their abusers. They may also tell the victims that their abusers are good people, or that the abuse is not as bad as it seems. They may even suggest that these abused women go back to their abusers and try harder to make things work.

- They feel responsible for the abuse or believe that it happens because of alcohol or drug use. They may believe that their abusers just can't control their anger. An abusive man will often tell his victim that no one else will ever love her as he does. Her self-esteem becomes dependent on his attention, and she tells herself that she can handle the abuse, figuring it's better to be with an abuser who "loves" her than to be alone and never again be loved.

- They experience episodes of physical violence in relatively short bursts, after which their batterers become gentle and loving, promising to change for good. This alternating cycle confuses victims, who see their batterers as loving partners some—even most—of the time. The batterers may convince their victims that they will change and that the relationship will get better. Victims don't want the relationship to end; they just want the violence to end.

- They witnessed fighting in their homes while they were growing up. If this is true of a victim, it makes it easier for her to accept violence as "okay." Most abusers learn violence from their own families. If both the abuser and the victim grew up in homes where violence was frequent, it may forge a bond of common experience between them that makes separation more difficult.

- They feel needed by their abusers and feel capable of helping them change.

- They feel that if they could only change and stop making mistakes, their abusers would be satisfied and stop hurting them. They blame themselves and their own "imperfections."

- They have difficulty knowing what really constitutes abuse. They may sense that their relationships are bad, but they fail to see a connection between the abuse and the bad relationships. They may identify their batterers' substance abuse, money problems, or stress outside the relationship as the real problem. These women may not know that they have the right to feel safe and to live without the threat of violence.

The majority of abused women eventually leave their abusers, but leaving an abuser is a process, not an event. A woman may make several attempts to leave her abuser before she is ultimately successful. Leaving an abuser before she is ready or leaving without ample resources and support will often result in a woman's returning to her abuser. It takes a great deal of resolve, energy, and courage to leave an abusive relationship for good.

2

"It's Tough Being One in a World Made for Two"

ॐ

Deborah's Story

Meet Deborah, who has an incapacitating fear of being alone. "I didn't really notice until after I left James for the first time how frightening being alone was for me," she said. "As a teen and even in college, I shared time with my girlfriends and my sorority sisters. One by one, friends got married and left the group, but the rest of us still had each other for support.

"When I tried to leave my sixteen-year marriage, all my girlfriends were married or remarried and in their own relationships. My family members had scattered and my parents were gone. As a woman alone without her husband, it seemed that I made my married friends feel uncomfortable around me. Many of them had been friends with both of us. Once the secret of his abuse was out, their loyalties were split. Most felt that they must take sides or at least distance themselves. A woman alone created an odd number—or someone who might tempt husbands in an already secretly shaky marriage. All of this added to my sense of alienation."

She continued, "Everywhere I looked or went, I felt like the odd person out. At the park, there were couples, groups of friends, and families. The same went for church. Small indications of affection between couples only made me feel worse. They were taunting red flags of what I had chosen to give up. Not yet single, I did not fit in at parties for singles or couples. I also felt uncomfortable getting a table for one at restaurants. The nights became longer, the silence of my small apartment heavier. As the ticking of the wall clock seemed to get louder, I panicked! Loneliness, I decided, would eat me alive. I could die and no one would know or miss me! I didn't feel like I belonged anywhere. *In spite of his abuse, when I was with him I still felt a sense of belonging.* Frankly, I was deciding which was worse—my overwhelming loneliness or his abuse."

The Powerful Fear of Solitude

> ℘
>
> The fear of loneliness can prevent you from leaving a bad situation.

Fear of being alone is a powerful force. It can cause you to make decisions you would not otherwise make. The fear of loneliness can prevent you from leaving a bad situation, or it can propel you into another unhealthy relationship.

A group of psychology majors at a private college sent out a questionnaire to graduates of that college in order to garner research for their thesis project. The questionnaire asked these graduates about their careers, lifestyles, and home lives. Of the women who responded and had been married during their senior year of college or just after graduating, 42 percent reported that they had married out of a sense of fear. They had feared not finding anyone to marry once they left college. The thought of loneliness had prompted them to marry the nearest interested man rather than waiting to ascertain whether another man might make a more suitable spouse. For many, their marriages had not lasted or were in trouble when the survey was taken. In retrospect, many of these women, now older and wiser, confessed that they should have listened to their inner voices—voices that had urged them to wait.

The prospect of loneliness can be intimidating. If you've been married and are accustomed to mingling in society as a couple, you may feel as if the social environment is hostile toward single people, which makes it difficult to break away from your spouse or partner.

You've experienced emotional and physical intimacy. Now, the idea of being "just one," paired with the grave responsibility of stepping away—even from a destructive relationship—horrifies you. Weighing all the possibilities and consequences, you may choose to forgo loneliness, even if it means risking further abuse. If you feel that you can't go on without your partner or husband in your life—which is probably what he has told you—you've become convinced that you're incapable of living alone. His intimidating tactics of control will continue to eat away at your inner core. The revolving door of abuse will never stop *until you make a final decision to leave.*

Most of the names in this book have been changed for obvious reasons. However, Christina O'Neil (Miss Nevada 2003) gave permission to use her name and her story.

Christina's Story, Part Two

In order to free herself from the trap of abuse, Christina had to overcome her fear of being alone. Overcoming the fear of solitude is no easy thing, but Christina's counselor taught her a technique that is largely responsible for making her the strong, intelligent, self-reliant woman she is today. Christina's counselor told her that she needed to practice "sitting with the tiger." This was her explanation of this technique: During the Stone Age, when now extinct creatures such as the woolly mammoth and saber-toothed tiger still existed, humans were rarely alone; they knew that being in groups decreased their chances of attack by the saber-toothed tiger. Today, though we are no longer threatened by actual saber-toothed cats, we are still threatened by our own metaphoric saber-toothed tigers— whatever debilitating fears prowl around the periphery of our minds and threaten to eat us up. But if you sit with your "tiger"—if you spend time with your fear, so to speak—it will eventually cease to scare you.

Christina was taught to sit with her "tiger," the fear of solitude, by actually sitting by herself. During these times of solitude, she could have no companionship or entertainment whatsoever—not even television shows, music, books, or telephone calls. She was told to do this as long as she could stand it. At first, she could sit for only about five minutes at a time; if she sat alone any longer, she started feeling like she was going to die. She gradually increased the time interval, still feeling the fear but beginning to realize that it wasn't as scary as she had originally thought. Before long, Christina was going to lunch by herself and feeling content about it. She realized that she had a lot of control over her well-being, and she began to feel a sense of inner peace.

> ❧
> Christina learned how to love herself, how to say no, and how to trust her instincts.

In addition to learning to be alone without fear, Christina learned how to love herself, how to say no, and how to trust her instincts. She shares her lessons here:

"My counselor told me that I needed to do something for myself and report back to her what I'd done. Believe it or not, this was hard for me. Somehow, I didn't feel deserving. I started with something simple. I got a manicure and began to feel good about my hands. Then, I began to take time to make some of my favorite, healthier foods. Immediately, I began to feel better."

Learning to say no was more difficult for Christina. "I had a terrible time saying no to anyone," she said. "I would agree to help people, even if it meant putting my own obligations on hold. My counselor told me to practice saying no. It began with simple things. If I were shopping at the grocery store and I wanted plastic instead of paper, I would speak up for myself." Slowly, Christina began to feel better about getting what she really wanted instead of always "giving in." Christina has learned to say no when she needs to without feeling guilty. She finally feels worthy enough to have her own needs met in addition to meeting the needs of others.

After an abusive relationship that lasted five years, Christina found it difficult to start dating again. She was afraid that what had happened in the past might occur again with future boyfriends. But she was instructed to get out there, watch for warning signs, and trust her instincts. Christina was looking for a man who respected women, so on the first or second date, she would ask questions about his family. If she received positive answers that indicated he cared about his family, she felt good about continuing the relationship. If the answers were negative, though—especially concerning female family members—this response sent up a red warning flag, and Christina would end that relationship then and there.

Unfortunately, she did encounter some disturbing men, some who used crass language and made suggestive remarks that embarrassed her. In these cases, she waited no more than fifteen minutes to excuse herself and end the dates. She stuck to her values and learned that there were decent, honorable men in the world. Christina eventually found what she was looking for in a relationship, and she accepted this man's marriage proposal. Her new fiancé loves his family, treats Christina and her sister with respect, and has never raised one red flag. They planned a summer marriage.

Christina's final piece of advice is *not to rush into anything*. She went through three years of counseling but called the experience entirely worthwhile. She has learned that she can be both alone and in love and be safe.

How to Listen to Your Hurting Friend

Unless you are a professionally trained therapist, do not attempt to provide therapy. Do, however, provide support and teach her that no one deserves to be abused. There is no excuse for abuse, and there are many places where she can receive help.

It may be very hard for women to talk about issues of abuse with males. Safety is the primary concern.

- **Believe her!** If she tells you that she is being abused, do not question her truthfulness. Remember that she is probably understating the violence and glossing over the gory details. What you hear may be just the beginning.

- **Confidentiality is crucial.** Obtain her consent in writing before you tell anyone else about the abuse. As you obtain her permission for disclosure, use this opportunity to encourage and empower her to make contacts for herself. Offer the use of your phone or computer. This allows you the opportunity to be supportive throughout the process while also letting her make her own decisions and seek her own help.

- **Do not disclose information** about the victim to the batterer. Be aware that many people who batter others feel a need to control them. Someone who batters may desire to control not only his victim, but also anyone willing to help her, such as a counselor, clergy member, friend, or other individual.

- **Validate her feelings** and affirm her courage in bringing her problem to you. You may be the first person whom she has approached, and you should assure her that she was right to do so.

- **Ask direct, specific questions.** Even if a victim admits that her partner hits, slaps, and punches her and calls her names, she may not acknowledge specifically that "violence" is going on in the relationship. By being direct, you are telling her that it is okay for her to discuss this difficult issue. By being specific, you help her to identify behavior that may be abusive and acknowledge it as such.

- **Listen to her** and comfort her without physically touching her. To touch her may bring painful memories to mind and cause her to withdraw rather than open up to you.

- **Make sure she knows that violence is unacceptable.** Convey the fact that it is against the law.

- **Unequivocally denounce the violence.** No one deserves to be abused. Do not ask her what she did to provoke it. She is in no way responsible for causing the abuse.

- **Make sure she's safe.** Deal efficiently and effectively with safety issues pertinent to this person.

- **Tell her she is not alone.** Too many suffer in silence, afraid to speak up because they don't realize how common their plight truly is.

- **Present her with options** from which to choose. Many battered women find it difficult to see options, much less act on them. Some of these options may include individual counseling sessions, support groups, divorce, or other legal aid, such as assistance in obtaining a protective order.

- **Support her decision** to act or not to act. She must be allowed to make changes in her own time, even if you are convinced that she should be doing something different or acting immediately. She probably has someone at home who is already telling her what to do and when to do it. Encourage her to verbalize and act on her own decisions.

How Can I Help My Friend?

- **Become informed.** Gather all the information you can find about domestic violence. Contact programs in your area that assist battered women and their children. These programs not only offer women safety, but they also provide advocacy, support, and other needed services.

- **Lend a sympathetic ear.** Letting your friend know that you care and are willing to listen may be the best help you can offer. Don't force the issue, but instead allow her to confide in you at her own pace. Keep your mind open and listen closely to what she tells you. Do not blame her for what's happening; never belittle her fears or her potential danger. Remember that your friend must make her own decisions about her life. Focus on supporting her right to make her own choices. Sometimes, your own feelings about domestic violence may make it difficult for you to confront the situation. Contact your local domestic violence hotline or program to discuss your concerns with the staff. Advocates of battered women can be excellent sources of support for both you and your friend.

- **Guide her to community services.** When she asks for advice about what she should do, share with her privately the information you've gathered. Let her know that she is not alone; assure her that caring people are available and eager to help her. Encourage her to seek the assistance of battered women's advocates at the local domestic violence hotline or program, and assure her that any information she shares with them will be kept strictly confidential. Many battered women first seek the advice of marriage counselors, psychiatrists, or clergy members, but not all helping professionals are fully aware of the special circumstances of abused women. If the first person she contacts is not helpful, encourage her to find assistance elsewhere, or she may grow discouraged and stop her search altogether.

- **Focus on her strengths.** Battered women live with emotional abuse in addition to physical and sexual abuse. Your friend is probably told continually by her abuser that she is a poor or inadequate woman, companion, and mother. If she receives no positive reinforcement from outside the home to counteract these negative statements, she may begin to believe she can't do anything right and that there really is something wrong with her. Give her the emotional support and positive encouragement she needs. Help her to explore and develop her strengths and skills. Emphasize that she *deserves* a life free from violence.

- **Through your actions, show your friend that you are there for her.** Provide whatever help you can, whether transportation, child care, financial assistance, or another form of help.

- **Listen without judging.** Many victims believe the negative things their abusers say about them. They may feel blameworthy, ashamed, inadequate, and afraid. You may be the only person who listens to her without returning criticism and judgment.

- **Tell her that the abuse is not her fault.** Explain that violence—physical, verbal, emotional, or sexual—is never acceptable in a relationship.

- **Make sure she knows she is not alone.** Every year, millions of people of every race, age, and religion are victims of domestic violence. Emphasize that help is available for her, just as it is available for the millions of others suffering similar abuse. Let her know that domestic violence tends to get worse and increase in frequency, and that it rarely goes away on its own.

- **Explain that this form of abuse is a crime** and that she can seek help from the courts and the police.

- **Suggest she develop a safety plan in case of an emergency.** It is a good idea to keep money, important documents, a change of clothes, and an extra set of keys in a safe place, such as with a nearby friend or at the home of a trusted neighbor.

- **Think about ways you might feel comfortable helping the person.** If she decides to leave her relationship, she may need financial assistance or a place to store her belongings. Think about offering your home as a place to stay, loaning her money, or making another significant sacrifice in order to help her recover.

What if she wants to remain in the relationship? It is important to understand that there are many reasons that people remain in or return to abusive relationships. In many cases, the victim fears for her life. She also may want her children to grow up with both parents. She may feel guilty, believing the abuse to be her own fault. Whatever your friend's reason for staying in an abusive relationship, it is important that you support her and continue to encourage her to live a life free of violence. Don't give up on her—your continued support may eventually help her to make a life-saving decision.

3

"At Least He's a Good Father"

❧

Barbara's Story

Barbara thought she had it all when she married Lee. However, living with Lee was like living with two different people. There was the doting, loving father to their nine-year-old son and six-year-old twin daughters. Behind closed doors, though, the "other" Lee turned cruel and evil toward Barbara.

In college, Barbara had taken marriage enrichment classes. She remembered what they had taught her: that love is a decision and that loving feelings follow that decision. Years later, in her moments of confusion and pain, it seemed to her that Lee had decided to love their children and to stop loving her. Every one of his words and actions was evidence of this decision. His contradictory behavior escalated into a heartbreaking, schizophrenic experience that ultimately shattered their marriage.

The abuse started when their twin daughters were two years old. Lee suddenly became overly protective of the children, referring to them as "mine." He became highly critical of how Barbara parented them. Nothing she did was quite right. He became paranoid about minute details—he blew up whenever Barbara took their children to the park. He insisted that they wear hats at all times. If they were playing in the yard at home, Barbara had to remain out in the yard with them. They were permitted exposure to no more than twenty minutes of sunshine and fresh air each day. The children's diets were under Lee's constant scrutiny, too.

Barbara's marriage to Lee was full of harsh criticism and impossible demands. No matter what she did, it wasn't satisfactory. She tried constantly to be the perfect wife and mother, but she never measured up as adequate in her husband's eyes.

Lee's verbal abuse escalated when the twins started kindergarten. His verbal abuse graduated to physical abuse, and he began to punch Barbara. Agonizing about what to do, Barbara kept saying to herself, *At least he's a good father.* She knew that if she left Lee, he would fight hard to keep the children. She feared that if he lost any control over the children, his abuse would escalate even more.

> ❧
> To outsiders and family members alike, it often appears that an abused woman is simply an unhappy, ungrateful person looking for sympathy and attention.

When Barbara finally told her mother about Lee's abusive behavior, she, too, responded, "At least he's a good father." She considered Lee a good catch, so she downplayed the abuse and urged her daughter, "Look how he treats the children. Really, Barbara, he can't be that bad! I think you just need to try harder to please him. Just be a good wife and mother and everything will be fine." By blinding herself to Barbara's misery, Barbara's mother unwittingly kept her daughter in a deadly trap. To outsiders and family members alike, it often appears that an abused woman is simply an unhappy, ungrateful person looking for sympathy and attention.

Barbara finally confided in a friend, who then confronted Lee about the abuse. Lee admitted that he had a temper but then blamed Barbara, saying, "She's self-centered. She should stop upsetting the family and setting off my temper. I'm a good father and a good provider—what else does she want?"

Lee was furious that Barbara had shared their personal business with "outside" friends. He screamed, "Leave! You can get out… but you'll never take the children!" Terror-stricken by this prospect, Barbara stayed with her husband. She continued to suffer so that she wouldn't lose her children

Perceived Dependency as Motivation to Stay

Economic dependency can be a powerful motivator that drives women back to their abusers. If you returned for this reason, it may be that without him, you and your children would face severe financial hardship. If you're a mother, the prospect of raising children on your own can further cloud your thinking. You may even choose to stay and endure the abuse so that your children will have financial security. Often, when a victim seeks refuge at a women's shelter, the first thing she says is, "How can I get by financially if I leave him for good? I must support my kids." This is a legitimate and real concern.

Dr. Lenore Walker, author of *The Battered Woman*, performed a study of four hundred thirty-five women. She found that 34 percent of them had no access to a checking account and 27 percent had no access to cash. Are you one of those women who stayed with an abuser or went back to him because you didn't think you could support yourself financially? If you still feel that way, do you wonder how you will acquire education and job skills necessary to keep a job? Has your partner threatened to withhold support, interfere with your job, or ruin your credit rating? Economic insecurity is a heavy burden. Do you find yourself weighing the alternatives—abuse or financial insecurity—and trying to decide which is worse?

You may stay or return after reminding yourself, *At least he's a good father*. If you have children and you're living with domestic violence, you may feel that you've made your bed and now have to lie in it. You rationalize. You may choose to risk the abuse again for the sake of financial security.

You think that by keeping the family together, you're protecting the children. In reality, leaving may be the only way to protect them. Maybe you're afraid that if you leave, your husband will redirect his anger at the children—and you may be right. You may be willing to take the abuse yourself, but seeing your children suffer abuse will usually compel you to leave.

Barbara and Tina have two different stories about the impact of domestic violence on their children.

Tina's Story

Tina's story is equally as painful as Barbara's. Though she was not married to an abuser, her mother was, and the memories haunt her still. Tina's mother had gotten pregnant out of wedlock. She finally married the baby's father, who became a pastor. Tina thought that his position as a pastor would make her father a kind, decent person. Instead, he had continual affairs with women of all ages from his congregation. When Tina's mother tried to confront him about these adulterous acts, he became defensive and began abusing her verbally to silence her. The verbal abuse escalated before turning into physical abuse.

Tina's father had forced her mother to work in his parents' restaurant, but he collected and kept all of her paychecks. He wouldn't provide transportation for her to go to and from work, so she had to walk. One day, Tina's father knocked his wife unconscious and hid her in the restaurant's walk-in freezer. By the grace of God, someone opened the freezer door and found Tina's mother before it was too late.

Witnessing her father's violence and volatility toward her mother naturally devastated Tina, who was five years old when her parents first separated. No matter where she and her mother went to escape her father, he always managed to find them. He insisted on taking Tina away from her mother, and she stayed in his custody through several remarriages. He molested his stepdaughters, but he didn't molest Tina—he let his friends molest her.

Tina's father always got away with the abuse. It was a shameful secret the family kept concealed, and even Tina's mother didn't know the degree to which her daughter suffered. This was due in part to her ex-husband's threats to kill her should she try to take Tina away from him. When Tina was twelve years old, she ran away from her father and reunited with her mother, who hid Tina at the home of a family member.

Later, Tina said that she could have testified against her father, but she feared for her life and chose not to. Many years later, he threatened to kill his own grandson if Tina ever said anything.

Tina's mother still blames herself for staying in her marriage as long as she did. She knows it inflicted incredible damage on her daughter, but she felt numb and incapable of making the decision to leave. She was also living in a state of constant fear. Tina's mother never remarried because she was desperately afraid of men and what they could do to her.

Even after her parents' divorce and her father's serial remarriages, Tina's father could not let go of her mother. He broke in to her home, tied her to a chair, and rigged up a gun so that it would fire at her when the phone rang. Tina's mother managed to get loose, though, and her life was spared again. Her ex-husband was finally arrested, prosecuted, and put in prison, where he died.

The healing process is an ongoing journey for Tina. She tries to bring hope to other women by speaking at churches and community groups.

The Effects of Abuse on Future Generations

Studies show that even if children do not witness the abuse, *they do feel it*. The following results can be expected when children live in abusive environments:

- Children come to believe that physical and verbal abuse is the norm for conflict resolution. They model the behavior they see and practice it on each other.

- Sons will often treat their mothers, their sisters, and—later— their wives in the same way they saw their fathers treat their mothers. They will exhibit disrespect and deny being in the wrong in the same way their fathers did, often name-calling with the same words and abusing with the same behaviors as their fathers.

- An opposite scenario can also occur. As young boys become aware of their fathers' abusive treatment of their mothers, they may try to protect them. Prisons are full of young men who have killed their fathers, stepfathers, or mothers' boyfriends for terrorizing their mothers.

- Daughters may come to believe that abuse is normal, which often leads to an unhealthy acceptance, tolerance, and even perpetuation of abuse in future relationships.

- The painful and destructive cycle of violence often continues from generation to generation until someone chooses to break it.

Clinicians often discover from talking with children who grew up in abusive environments that they saw and heard a lot more than their parents thought they had. Parents' attempts to hide the abuse are often futile, and most children from abusive environments can give detailed, accurate accounts of what was going on within their homes.

Vanessa's Story

Vanessa's story shows the long-term effects of abuse on a child. Now in her seventies, Vanessa has suffered a variety of physical ailments throughout her life. As a baby, she was hospitalized several times with severe constipation or diarrhea. At age nineteen, she was diagnosed with rheumatoid arthritis, and the medications she has had to use throughout the years have produced adverse side effects and reactions. As Vanessa's arthritic pain was becoming less and less bearable, a rheumatic specialist inquired about her childhood.

Vanessa told the doctor about her alcoholic father's rampages; he beat her mother to the point that she took her daughter and fled. Years of financial hardship followed, Vanessa said, but it was better than living in fear and putting up with the battering. Although Vanessa had been diagnosed with rheumatoid arthritis, this doctor could find no conclusive evidence that she ever had this disease. He inferred that her symptoms stemmed instead from her emotional reactions to the abuse she had endured throughout childhood.

Other young people have witnessed horrendous acts of abuse by fathers, stepfathers, or mothers' boyfriends. These scenes incite a variety of intense psychological and physical problems not unlike Vanessa's. Even though most abuse is initially directed at a female partner, studies show that it often extends to target the children, as well. As I have mentioned previously, even the unborn suffer: the number one cause of death among pregnant women is murder by their husbands.

The Reasons for Staying Change in Nature, not in Complexity

If you have remained in a violent relationship, you may have rationalized your reasons for staying, which may or may not involve children. Your reasons for staying will often change over time, too. Examine the below reasons frequently given to justify staying. Do some of the following resonate with your own experience?

At first, you stay because:

- You love him.

- You believe that you can reason with him.

- You feel ashamed and embarrassed.

- You made a marriage vow you don't want to break.

- You believe that he's capable of changing.

- You believe you can control his rage if you just try harder.

- You believe that if you can convince him that you love him, his abusive behavior will stop.

Later on, you stay because:

- You love him, but less.

- You're under pressure from family members and friends to stay.

- You still hope that he'll get help and change.

- You've become afraid of being alone.

- You still believe that he loves and needs you.

- You don't think that you could support yourself financially.

- You would fear for your life if you were to leave.

Finally, you stay because:

- You fear him; he's become all-powerful and inescapable in your eyes.

- Your self-esteem is lower than ever.

- You believe him when he says that no one else will love you as he does.

- You want to protect yourself and your children, whom he's threatened to kill if you leave.

- You don't want to be responsible for his death, and he's threatened to take his own life if you leave.

- You don't know how to survive without him.

- You feel extremely confused, even guilty.

- You have a hard time making even the smallest of decisions.

- You feel depressed, sometimes so much so that you can't even get out of bed in the morning.

- You feel like your life is out of control.

- You feel hopeless and helpless.

- You can't see any options.

- You have multiple physical ailments or emotional problems.

- You may be numbed by the medicines you're taking for these physical and emotional problems and are thus unable to think rationally.

- You may even feel suicidal.

Becky's Story

Becky, who is nearing age sixty, is a speaker about domestic violence and related issues. She grew up in an environment of domestic abuse, and in her home, the trigger was alcohol—both her mother and father were alcoholics. One day, during her senior year of high school, Becky's fourteen-year-old brother came home after finishing his paper route to find their mother's dead body in the garage. His father had just beaten her severely before shooting her in the head.

All three of Becky's siblings grew up to be alcoholics. Her younger brother committed suicide in his mid-twenties. Her sister became a workaholic. Becky herself chose not to have children because she was afraid of her own violent temper.

Becky sees the urgent need for speaking out against domestic violence. When she speaks to groups, she realizes that most people from violent homes are still hurting—at least emotionally if not also physically. By raising awareness about domestic violence and speaking about related issues, she is using her life to make a positive difference for others who have come from families like hers.

Laura's Story

I cannot overemphasize the truth that no one ever *deserves* emotional or physical abuse. The experience of Laura, Sarah's mother, whom I introduced at the beginning of this book, is grossly unnerving, particularly because she believed that she deserved the abusive treatment her husband was giving her. She said her situation was a textbook example of domestic violence: it was a continual cycle of honeymoon, tension, explosion, and honeymoon again. The verbal abuse began with demeaning remarks and cruel potshots. Laura allowed her husband's judgments and opinions to shape her own reality. She grew increasingly isolated from friends and family to the point that it seemed she had nowhere to turn for emotional support or validation of her feelings.

Nothing in Laura's life could have prepared her for what she would face in her marriage. She'd grown up in a middle-class home in the metropolitan area of Washington, D.C., and earned her bachelor of arts degree with honors from a small, liberal arts college in Virginia. After graduating, she worked in a prosecutor's office, so she knew a lot about domestic violence. She just never expected it to touch her own life. She felt sorry for the women who came into her office seeking legal assistance or divorce proceedings. Laura became frustrated when women dropped charges against their boyfriends or husbands. To her, domestic violence was a no-brainer. She thought, *He hits you, you walk away. He hits, you leave. It's simple!* Only when Laura suffered domestic abuse herself did she realize how far from simple it is.

Leaving an abuser is simple until he's your husband and you have children who are involved. It's simple until you've taken a vow to love, honor, and cherish him for as long as you both shall live. It's simple until there are mortgages and car payments.

As I said before, Laura's husband's abuse went from verbal abuse to physical violence, compelling Laura to seek the help of a domestic violence counselor at Harbor House in Orlando, Florida. There, she learned that domestic violence is all about *power and control*. Laura's husband was trying to have *power over* her. He threatened and intimidated her, and even when she got away, she didn't distance herself and her daughter enough from her violent ex-husband.

If you are an abused woman who is also a mother, Laura urges you not to take the safety of your own children for granted. She says emphatically, "I ask anyone who fears for her own safety to think twice and then twice more before dismissing the possibility that her child could become a victim." After years of personal reflection, Laura is still wondering what she could have done to prevent Sarah's death. She never imagined that her ex-husband could kill his own daughter.

Well-meaning people have asked Laura why she stayed with an abusive husband, then kept returning to him. Looking back, Laura says, "It would be easy to paint a picture of an evil husband who had no redeeming qualities. It would not be accurate. If that had been the case, I never would have married him in the first place."

Losing a child is one of the worst things any parent can endure. The thought that you could have done something to prevent your child's death makes the tragedy even more unbearable. This type of introspection has plagued Laura for years. She made this appeal: "It would be easy to turn our backs and say, 'It is not *my* problem.' But the reality is that someone you know—at work, at school, at church, or in your neighborhood—is currently facing an abusive situation. If a woman came to you for help, would you know what to do?"

The Impact of Domestic Abuse on Children

Please note the typical effects on children exposed to domestic violence, listed by age group:

Under Two Years of Age

- Response to loud noises and other unexpected events shows increased fear (crying, "startle reflex," and so forth).

- Developmental delays (takes more time than most to learn to crawl, walk, talk, and so forth).

- Nightmares and sleep disturbances.

Between Two and Five Years of Age

- Regressive behavior (loss of progress made with toilet training, use of baby talk, desire for bottle or pacifier, and so forth).

- Somatic problems (stomach aches, pains, and other complaints that have no apparent cause).

- Nightmares and sleep disturbances.

- Hypervigilance and "clingy" behavior.

- Repetitive play that acts out the domestic violence witnessed or experienced.

- Increased violence toward siblings.

- Cruelty to animals.

- Developmental delays (slow to learn colors, ABCs, and so forth).

- Decrease in playfulness and spontaneous behavior.

- Feelings of responsibility for violence in family; belief that if they behaved better, the violence would not occur.

- Increased dependence on primary caregiver (usually the non-abusive parent).

Between Six and Twelve Years of Age

- Increased problems at school.

- Frequent misbehavior and increased obstinacy (lying, aggression, stealing, truancy, and so forth).

- Labeled by teachers or counselors as having attention-deficit disorder or learning disabilities.

- Tendency to withdraw and be reclusive.

- Assumption of the role of "family help" or rescuer.

- Redirection of inner rage (pent-up anger) at the abused parent. The child is afraid to direct his or her anger at the abuser for fear of retaliation from the abuser.

- Development of an inflated sense of responsibility (becoming a "little adult").

- Learned disrespect of the victim of domestic violence because she tolerates the abuse.

- Confusion of love and violence from learning that people hit those whom they love.

- Development of emotional problems, such as depression.

Between Twelve and Eighteen Years of Age

- Aggressive behavior (prompted by the belief that violence can solve problems and is effective in controlling others).

- Severe behavior and emotional problems (running away, theft, depression, anxiety, and so forth).

- Belief in rigid gender roles; strong convictions about what behaviors are permissible for each gender.

- Involvement in dating violence, either as a perpetrator or a victim.

- Self-destructive behavior (abuse of drugs and/or alcohol, eating disorders, sexual promiscuity, suicide attempts, and so forth).

- Increased risk of teen pregnancy; increased likelihood of early marriage (two perceived "escape routes" from parents).

- Increased risk of suicide and homicide (killing the abuser).

- Development of boundaries that are emotionally closed or excessively open.

- Distrust of most authority figures, possibly of all adults.

The effects of domestic violence on children who witness it are dramatic. Its insidious influence can be serious and longstanding, regardless of whether the children have themselves been abused by a violent parent. The following is a summary of common consequences.

- Children will sometimes attempt to intervene, putting themselves in danger of physical harm. In one study, 63 percent of males between eleven and twenty years of age who committed homicide murdered the men who were abusing their mothers.[33] Children often feel guilty that they were not able to prevent the violence and sometimes feel they were somehow to blame for it.

- Depression, impaired trust, and low self-esteem are common among children who witness domestic violence.

- Witnessing violence in the home often leads to behavioral problems in children. Children will typically develop behavior that is predominantly aggressive or submissive, and this is often determined by the parent with whom they identify: the abuser (aggressive) or the victim (submissive).

- Emotional problems may ensue, including, but not limited to, anxiety disorders, phobias, learning problems, slowed social development, and other developmental delays.

---

[33] "Domestic Violence Awareness Institution," The Public Training Institute, 2000.

- Children may develop academic or behavioral problems at school, engage in drug or alcohol abuse, or exhibit delinquent behavior.

- Research points to a strong tendency for the cycle of violence to continue into the next generation. Children raised in violent homes are at a higher risk of getting involved in violent relationships as teens or adults. Boys who witness their fathers' violent treatment of their mothers are ten times more likely than boys from nonviolent homes to abuse their wives when they are adults.[34]

---

[34] Family Violence: Interventions for the Justice System, 1993.

4

"I Don't Know Who I Am Anymore"

↶

Do you sometimes wonder whether you're just imagining it all? Do you wonder to yourself, *Am I losing my mind? He told me that it would never happen again. But it happens over and over again. What's wrong with me? I feel like I'm going crazy!* You may look in the mirror and ask yourself, *Who is this person with the bruised face? I used to be pretty. I don't even look like me anymore.*

Gay's Story

Gay's relationship with her abusive spouse started early in their marriage. "I thought he was right for me. I was twenty-two, and I'd fallen madly in love with him," she said. "He was a strong man and I thought he was mature. I didn't see any red flags before we were married."

Gay vividly remembers the trigger that set off her husband for the first time. It happened when "I had my own opinion about something," Gay said. "He didn't hit me with his hands; he hit me with his fist. I fought back. Then, he picked me up, threw me into the bedroom, and locked the door." Gay continued to go back to him, again and again. Why did she stay? Because she thought she loved her husband and felt sure he would change. Each time she fought back, she lost a little more of herself. Then, the blow that caused Gay to leave finally came. She recounted, "He gathered my long hair together at the back of my head. I heard my neck pop, and then he was sitting on my back. I thought he'd broken my neck. Within two days, I was gone, and this time, I never went back. I was not going to let this be the end of my life."

Eight months later, Gay's marriage was over. Some women in relationships like Gay's stay for years and years. Don't be one of them. Gay's experience inspired her to join the army, and today she is a career officer with the military police. She has reclaimed her personal power and says that she could not be happier.

Domestic Abuse Has No Age Limit

Our government uses a code of colors called the Homeland Security Advisory System to alert us about potential terror threats. Each color—green, blue, yellow, orange, and red—signifies an increasingly high degree of risk. There is no such color code, however, for the one in three American women who deals with terror in her own home, especially if she is part of the elder population.

Samantha serves on the board of directors for a women's center in Florida, where she also volunteers. She stresses the importance of *listening* to the hurting women and children, who "need a sounding board; they are very confused." Samantha also sees many cases of elder abuse. Often, women have lost their identities by the time they get up in years. Only a few decades ago, the trend was still for women to drop out of college or quit their jobs once they married. They took on the title of "Mrs." and lost their own identities in the process. Being stripped of an important part of their identities made them more likely to remain in bad marriages because they could see no other options.

Only in recent years has elder abuse received national attention. Approximately five million Americans aged sixty-five and over are abused by a relationship partner each year.[35] Some surveys sug-

---

[35] Legal Services for the Elderly, 2001, cited in "Elder Abuse, Neglect, and Exploitation" by Jason C. Charland, prepared for the Blaine House Conference on Aging, September 2006. Orono, Maine: The University of Maine Center on Aging.

gest that there are approximately 500,000 to 1,000,000 victims of this hidden epidemic each year. The public is largely unaware of domestic violence that occurs late in life, especially because of the private nature of the senior age group; they tend to experience shame and embarrassment that prevent them from sharing uncomfortable truths. They are a generation who grew up in a time when the wife took care of her family and did whatever her husband said. He was the boss, and if she didn't like something he said or did, she shut up and took it anyway. Most victims of late-life domestic violence don't know where to seek help, so their suffering often goes unreported. Fortunately, available resources are being made more accessible to this group. There is now a National Center on Elder Abuse in Washington, D.C. Call them or visit their Web site (www.ncea.aoa.gov) to learn about their outreach efforts and to access data and other resources.

We are still a long way from solving the tragic problem of elder abuse. More than fifteen years have passed since the U.S. House of Representatives last held hearings on this issue. We need to encourage our representatives to cosponsor acts that promote justice for elders. People need to recognize the scope and severity of this issue. Rep. Peter King (R-NY) remarked, "Older people who have been abused don't talk about it. Who are you going to tell if it's happening in your own home?" In addition to the silence of victims, the other major problem is that the legislation inevitably competes with other national priorities. The only question left to answer is: Why has it taken so long?

It is not easy for any abused woman to reveal in detail what she's been through. If your life has been shattered by abuse, you often feel that you've lost your sense of "self." Your partner may have threatened to harm you if you tell anyone about the abuse in your relationship. He probably denies everything, too. He lives in denial of his own responsibility, maintaining that it's entirely your fault. But don't be intimidated. It is vitally important for your health—and survival—to tell others about the abuse you suffer. Remember, the

> ❧
> Don't be intimidated. It is vitally important for your health—and survival—to tell others about the abuse.

authorities and counselors whose help you seek are legally obligated to keep your comments confidential.

The first time your gut tells you something isn't right, trust it. Nip the problem in the bud—even if the abuse is "mild," it will eventually grow and erupt into something unbearable. The good news is that you have at your disposal many resources that *can* help you.

Look for the Following Red Flags

- **Jealousy.** At the beginning of an abusive relationship, an abuser will always say that jealousy is a sign of love. Jealousy has nothing to do with love—it's a sign of possessiveness, and it comes from a lack of trust. He will question the woman about the people she talks to, accuse her of flirting, or act slighted when she spends time with family members, friends, or even her own children. As the jealousy progresses, he may call her frequently throughout the day or drop by unexpectedly at her home or place of work. He may refuse to let her maintain her job for fear that she will meet someone else to whom she is attracted. He may even act like a sort of spy, monitoring her car's mileage or her telephone minutes, for example, or asking her friends to keep an eye on her activities and then report back to him.

- **Controlling behavior.** At first, the batterer will say that he's behaving this way because he is concerned for the woman's safety, for her need to manage her time well, or for her need to make good decisions. He will be angry if the woman is "late" coming home from the store or returning from an appointment. He will question her closely about where she went, what she did, and to whom she spoke. As he grows increasingly controlling, he may not allow the woman to make any decisions regarding household management, her wardrobe, or where they attend church. He may keep all the money out of reach, commandeering her paychecks and allocating her salary as he pleases. He may require her to obtain his permission to leave the house or even the room.

- **Quick involvement.** Many battered women knew or dated their abusers for less than six months before the two were engaged, married, or living together. A man with abusive tendencies may come in like a whirlwind, claiming, "You're the only person I could ever talk to; I've never felt loved like this by anyone." He will pressure the woman to commit to the relationship in such a way that if she later desires to decrease involvement or end the relationship altogether, she will feel extremely guilty, like she's letting him down.

- **Unrealistic expectations.** An abusive man will expect his partner to meet all of his needs. He demands that she be the perfect wife, mother, lover, or friend. He will say things like, "If you love me, I'm all you need, and you're all I need." She is supposed to take care of everything, from meeting his emotional and physical needs to keeping house, cooking, and cleaning.

- **Isolation.** The abuser tries to cut off all resources his partner might try to access or contact. If she has male friends, he calls her a "whore," and to avoid this designation she stops seeing them. If she has female friends, he calls her a "lesbian," and again, she cuts off contact. If she's close to her family, he says she's "tied to the apron strings." He accuses those people who usually support her of "causing trouble." He may want her to live with him in a remote location and without phone or Internet access. She might not be permitted to use a car, especially one that's reliable, and she also might be prohibited from working or attending school.

- **Displacement of blame for problems on other people.** If he is chronically unemployed, he either says someone is "doing me wrong" or someone is "out to get me." He may make mistakes and then blame the woman for upsetting him or keeping him from concentrating on his work. He will fault his partner for almost anything that goes wrong and try to make her feel guilty.

- **Denial of personal responsibility for emotions.** He will tell his partner, "You make me mad. You are hurting me by not doing what I want you to do. I can't help being angry because of you." His feelings of anger, dissatisfaction, and frustration are always her fault, according to him.

- **Hypersensitivity.** An abuser is usually quick to take offense or feel insulted. He will claim that his feelings are hurt when the reality is that he's mad; he will take the slightest of setbacks as a personal attack. He might rant and rave about the "injustice of it all"—things that have happened to him that are just part of living, such as being asked to work overtime, getting a traffic ticket, receiving requests to help with household chores, or being told that a behavior of his is annoying.

- **Cruelty to animals or children.** He may punish pets brutally or treat wild animals cruelly, showing insensitivity or apathy to their pain and suffering. He may expect children to do things above and beyond their abilities and become enraged when they fail, such as whipping a two-year-old for wetting a diaper. He may tease children or younger siblings until they cry. He may rule that children cannot eat at the dinner table with him; he may insist that they stay in their rooms all evening when he comes home from work. The sad truth is that 50 percent of men who beat their girlfriends or wives also beat these women's children.[36]

- **"Playful" use of force in sex.** Someone who takes abuse into the bedroom may enjoy throwing the woman and holding her down during sex. He may insist on acting out sexual fantasies in which the woman is helpless, which is a red flag indicating

---

[36] Straus and Gelles, *Physical Violence in American Families.*

that the idea of rape excites him. He may show little concern about whether the woman is in the mood to have sex, and if she seems reluctant, he will sulk or make threats to elicit her compliance. He may start having sex with the woman while she is still asleep or demand sex when she is ill or tired.

- **Verbal abuse.** The abuser says things that are meant to be cruel and hurtful. He degrades the woman, cursing her and cutting down her self-esteem by discrediting her skills and accomplishments. He will tell the woman that she is stupid, incompetent, and unable to function without him. To wear her down, he may even wake her up to abuse her verbally, thus preventing her from getting adequate amounts of quality sleep.

- **Abiding by and upholding rigid gender roles.** The abuser expects his female partner to serve him. He may order the woman to stay at home to cook, clean, and manage the household. He expects her to obey him always and do what he says, even if his orders are criminal in nature. Male abusers see women as inferior to men, hold them responsible for performing menial tasks, consider them to be stupid, and view them as incomplete without a relationship.

- **A Jekyll and Hyde personality.** His mood may change unpredictably and suddenly, causing confusion in his partner. One minute, he's friendly and kind; the next minute, he's exploding with anger. She may think that mental problems are to blame, but explosiveness and moodiness typify people who beat their partners and are related to other characteristics, such as hypersensitivity.

- **A history of battering.** The abuser may admit to having hit women in the past, but only because "they made me do it." His relatives, ex-girlfriends, or ex-wives may warn his current partner that he is abusive. Someone who is abusive will beat any woman he is with—if she sticks around long enough for the violence to begin. Abusive personalities are not caused by situations and circumstances, so don't expect that his changing jobs, moving to a new town, or marrying you will make him change for the better. Abusive tendencies are not conditional.

- **Threats of violence.** These include any threats of physical force the abuser uses with the intention of controlling his partner, such as "I'll slap your mouth off," "I'll kill you," or "I'll break your neck." He may try to put his partner at ease by assuring her, "Everybody talks like that." But it is neither common nor acceptable for people to threaten their partners.

- **Breaking/striking objects.** The abuser's violent behavior toward inanimate objects, especially treasured possessions of his partner, is used to terrorize the woman into submission. He may beat on the table with his fist and throw objects at or near her. Not only is this a sign of extreme emotional immaturity, but there is also great danger posed by a person who thinks he has the "right" to punish or frighten his girlfriend or wife.

- **Use of any kind of force during an argument.** The batterer will often use physical force against his partner, such as holding her down, restraining her so that she can't leave the room, or pushing and shoving her. He may hold her up against the wall and scream, "You *will* listen to me!"

Faith's Story

For most of her twenty-five years of marriage to her second husband, Faith experienced varying degrees of abuse. She was deeply in love with her husband, a formidable man who controlled her every move. As crazy as it sounds, even when he pointed a gun at her head and accused her of having an affair, she told him how much she loved him. Faith insisted that she had no idea she was being abused. "I didn't realize it at first. I didn't understand that he was controlling me. He never hit me, but I always felt like I was under his thumb. I had to show him all the receipts for purchases I had made. He checked the hour on them to see how much time I spent between getting off work and going home. I finally realized what was happening, but I still wanted to hold my family together. I made it look to other people like we had a happy, Christian home. I was lying to myself and to them. I did that for years."

A trip to their daughter's home was the beginning of the end. Faith's husband said he didn't want to make the trip, so Faith went alone. "I wasn't going to argue with him when he said he didn't want to go. When I came home, he yelled, 'Nobody's glad to see you!' He was huffing and puffing, furious with me. I started to fix something to eat, and he started accusing me of being with another man. He exclaimed, 'I found out about you and your man. His name is engraved on the countertop here.' Of course, there was no name on the counter. When I turned around, he was pointing the gun at my head. I screamed at him, 'I love you; why are you doing this to me?' He responded, 'You've been going somewhere, so just go where he is!' He picked up my purse and car keys and threw them at me. He told me to get out. I was so afraid. Where was I going to go? I drove to our daughter's home. I was so confused that I actually had a nervous breakdown. I wanted to commit suicide, but God walked me through it. I had a good friend who counseled me. She told me that suicide was not an option. I found out that I was not alone and that there are a lot of people who want to help. Now, I tell women, 'If he's trying to control you, get out of the relationship.' I should have left at least ten years before he pointed the gun at me. Because I didn't understand domestic violence, I almost lost my life. Now I know that nothing I could have done would have changed his behavior. I tried to turn myself inside out, twisting myself like a pretzel to please him, and nothing worked."

"Domestic Violence Isn't an Anger Problem"

Many people mistakenly believe that domestic violence stems from a problem with anger management. According to Diana Patterson, L.G.S.W., a social worker and violence prevention coordinator at the Mayo Clinic in Rochester, Minnesota, "Domestic violence isn't an anger problem. Batterers take their anger out on their intimate partner, but it's not really about anger. It's about trying to instill fear and wanting to have power and control in the relationship." Anger is simply one method the abuser uses to exert and maintain authority. He needs to feel power over his victim. Anger, sarcasm, the silent treatment, and name-calling are just a few of the methods he uses to achieve this power. Eventually, verbal and emotional abuse escalates into physical violence. At last, he has achieved his goal.

Christian's Story

Faith's daughter, Christian, continues the story from her own perspective. Like her first husband, Faith's second husband, Christian's stepfather, was abusive. When they were married, Christian says that her stepfather constantly degraded her mother. Every day, he would come home from work in a rage. In order to cope, her mother mastered the art of denial. Faith felt that she had to hold her second marriage together, whatever it took. He was her world; he was her sole source of love. Faith had been given up for adoption at a young age, and she was thereafter driven by a need for love and acceptance. She was always looking for a place to really belong.

After her stepfather pointed the gun at Faith, Christian was terrified. She was afraid that her mother would go back to him after this violent episode, and she felt like she was the mother, and her mother was the child—a complete role reversal.

After suffering a nervous breakdown and a minor stroke, Faith finally mustered the strength to leave her abusive husband. It was a strength that Christian had never before seen her mother display, but even after leaving him, Faith maintained that she loved her husband. When he was taken to jail, she went to pieces. It took time for Faith to recover from her nervous breakdown, but she eventually returned to work. The local victim's assistance program helped get Faith back on her feet. Mother and daughter are both grateful for the victim's assistance program, which they credit with saving Faith's life.

Christian admits that she became addicted to work, where she sought refuge from her tumultuous home life. By the age of nineteen, she was working three jobs. In her dysfunctional home, she was very unhappy, and the consequences of a difficult childhood followed her into adulthood. She frequently felt trapped, experiencing again the fears she felt even as a six-year-old.

Christian's stepfather was the only father and male role model she had known as a child, and she ultimately picked a husband who was almost exactly like her stepfather. She knew that she had married her stepfather, in essence, when she started to receive the same kind of treatment her mother had received. Faith had compromised her own dreams and suffered in so many ways, and Christian did not want to relive her mother's life.

She knew that she didn't have to repeat the patterns, and, armed with that knowledge, as well as with courage, she filed for divorce. Because she wasn't ashamed then, she doesn't have to be afraid now. Today, Christian is a successful entrepreneur with her own business. She has learned a great deal about people, and she wants to help everyone she can to live the best life, whatever that means to them.

Christian's life proves that there can be life after abuse. Today, she feels free and fulfilled, thanks to the strength her mother inspired. She is proud of her mother for finally leaving her abusive husband, and she says that her mother's strength gave her strength.

The research for this book came from hundreds of women whom I interviewed. However, I know a number of men who also have experienced abuse.

John's Story

It all started one summer. John was happily married with three children, and he had no clue that his marriage was in trouble. His wife began to make false accusations. She verbally abused him and called him every foul word in the book. They were actively involved in their church, and eventually they talked about their problems with the pastor. Still, her behavior did not change. To John's surprise, when guests joined them at their home for dinner one evening, his wife blew up at him in front of their guests. She accused him of orchestrating the entire visit behind her back, when in reality she had invited them in the first place. Their guests were concerned by her paranoid behavior.

John's job required him to travel, but he rearranged his work routine so that he would not have to leave his children alone with their mother in such a frightening, unhealthy environment. He wanted desperately to save his marriage, so much so that he resigned from his well-paying job to placate his wife's complaints about his frequent travels. But resigning was not good enough for her. Despite John's willingness to make sacrifices in order to repair the marriage, his wife filed for divorce—as well as a restraining order against John. He was completely baffled and confused, as he had never once threatened her or behaved violently. She was using the classic abuser's tactic of keeping the victim off balance and befuddled.

The verbal abuse escalated to physical abuse. It is sometimes hard to imagine, but certain women have physiques sturdy enough—and anger strong enough—to beat up on men. John's wife hit him in the chest so hard that their children started screaming for her to stop. But her violence continued; she kicked John and then pinned him on the floor. He could take her abuse no longer, so he wrenched free and called 9-1-1. When the police arrived, the children informed them that their father had never started any of the fights; it had always been their mother. The bruises that covered John corroborated his children's account, and John's wife was charged with domestic violence.

Now, John is divorced, though he never imagined it would happen to him. His son, who had always been a straight-A student, required counseling to recover from the family trauma. Years later, John met a beautiful Christian woman, and the two are planning a wedding.

Each year, 835,000 men are assaulted by their intimate partners, according to the National Violence against Women Survey.[37] Some

---

[37] Patricia Tjaden and Nancy Thoennes, "Full Report of the Prevalence, Incidence, and Consequences of Violence," National Institute of Justice and the Centers for Disease Control and Prevention, November 2000.

of these men have been kicked, bitten, hit, threatened, beat up, or attacked with a gun or a knife. Male victims who seek help are often ignored, ridiculed, and even accused by the authorities of having started the conflicts. Well-known historical and political figures also have been the victims of domestic violence. In his book *The Inner World of Abraham Lincoln*, Michael Burlingame examines the severe assaults that the sixteenth president suffered at the hand of his wife, Mary Todd Lincoln. *Abused Men: The Hidden Side of Domestic Violence* by Philip Cook shares the stories of dozens of abused men who were met with skepticism instead of the help they sought. When men have the courage to admit that their female partners have abused them, people rarely believe them. Because the preponderance of domestic violence is committed by men against women, it can be difficult to believe evidence that identifies the perpetrator as a female. If a male victim of domestic abuse calls a shelter to ask for help, the voice at the other end often does not take him seriously. However, according to Sen. Orrin Hatch (R-UT), "Men who have suffered violent attacks are eligible under current law to apply for services and benefits under the Violence against Women Act of 2000—whether it be for shelter space, counseling, or legal assistance." Vice President Joe Biden was largely responsible for the Act when he was in the Senate. He agreed with Sen. Hatch's statement, saying, "Nothing in the act denies services, programs, funding, or assistance to male victims of violence."

Regardless of this and other legislative attention, abused men are not taken seriously in most states. There is rampant discrimination by the federal and state governments, national domestic violence organizations, and state domestic violence coordinating councils against men who claim to suffer domestic abuse. In fact, there are only a few shelters in the United States that provide a full range of services to male victims. Most shelters are designed exclusively to harbor women who have left abusive men. Quite sadly, many abused men have simply stopped asking for help. Abused men need to receive "equal treatment under the law." The words of that basic constitutional right are boldly inscribed on the face of the U.S. Supreme Court building.

Ted's Story

Ted's mother told him that he looked angry in the photos taken of him when he was eight years old. Today, he has only vague memories of his father's beatings. When he was a little boy, his father would punch him in the head if he couldn't provide correct answers to questions about the Catholic religion. His father also threatened his mother and sister. He was a Jekyll and Hyde personality: slick salesman by day, fearsome father by night. During parent-teacher meetings at the Catholic school his children attended, the nuns loved Ted's father. They never questioned the origin of Ted's bruises, swollen lips, and red marks. Sometimes, Ted was beaten so badly that his mother called the police, but his father was skilled at making excuses the police could believe. They always left without filing any charges.

Finally, when Ted was twenty years old, his father punched him in the face so severely that Ted had to be taken to the emergency room in an ambulance. After this episode, Ted left home—and his mother, who now bore the brunt of her husband's abuse. Her parents were well-known in the community, and to preserve their good reputation, she tried to hide the abuse that was taking place in her home. Ted tried to tell his cousins what was happening, but they refused to believe him. Ted was the only person to whom his gentle mother could turn. Through the years, Ted would call the police whenever his father abused his mother. Still, the police would not take his reports seriously, and his mother never pressed charges.

Years later, when Ted was in his thirties, he returned home to protect his mother, knowing that his presence would likely be the only thing that would prevent his father from killing her. His father resented the close relationship Ted and his mother shared, and when Ted left home again at age thirty-four, his father began censoring phone conversations between the two of them. In the course of the final phone conversation Ted shared with his mother, she told him that his father would never allow her to see her son or talk to him again. After this revelation, the line went dead; Ted's father had pulled the phone cord out of the wall. His mother was a prisoner in her own home. Nine years passed with no communication between Ted and his mother, and it was through the Internet that Ted learned that his mother had died. No one except Ted knew what had really gone on behind closed doors.

During my interview with Ted, I asked him how his past had affected his present. He told me that anytime he undertakes a new project, he's always enthusiastic at the outset, but his interest wanes and he is never able to finish it. He went on to trace the roots of this issue, explaining that his father used to call him at work to harass him several times a day. Whenever the phone rang, Ted said, his body would jerk on impulse. He finally managed to overcome this jumpiness, but the process of learning to master it was a long, hard road. Ted said that he was unable to make commitments of any sort, whether signing a lease on an apartment or entering into a serious relationship. Today, Ted lives in a hotel, paying as he goes; there is no lease to sign, no contractual obligations for him to fulfill. Ted still has mood swings, but he says that they are decreasing in frequency and severity.

Of all the interviews I conducted, his was one of the most poignant. He told me that before age eight, he had been a happy, normal little boy. His memories from the first few years of his life are positive. Only recently has Ted, now in his mid-fifties, rediscovered the same enthusiasm for life that he felt before age eight. For years, he had been desperately shy, but he recently completed a public speaking course at the New School in Greenwich Village, New York, to overcome his timidity. Now, he even takes acting classes. He says that his goal is to draw upon the past to create a new present. Both his public speaking course and acting classes have proven therapeutic for Ted. His personality is gradually returning to that of the joyful little boy he was before the beatings began.

Monica's Story

Monica still finds it hard to believe that abuse could have happened to her. A starry-eyed Italian girl, she married Van, who was a handsome young man—Italian, too—from a wealthy family with a reputation for being "good Catholics." Monica thought that she had married very well. How wrong she was!

The terror began when Monica found out that she was pregnant and told her husband the news. She expected Van to be thrilled. Instead, he grew red-faced with anger and told her firmly that he did not want any children. Then, he shoved Monica repeatedly against the bedroom wall, hoping she would lose the baby. He succeeded. The force of the blows caused her to miscarry. As Monica lay bleeding in the hospital emergency room, she was too ashamed to tell the truth to Van's family doctor.

Monica felt desperate, but there had never been a divorce in her family, and she didn't want to be the first. *If Van feels so adamant about not having any kids, then I'll just have to give up my plans for motherhood*, she thought. When she told Van that she would submit to his wishes, his response was, "Just remember: don't let yourself get pregnant again!" He was blaming her—and warning her.

She remembered his threatening words every time they had sex. Lovemaking for Monica was anything but, and she lived in constant fear of becoming pregnant again. Sure enough, she got pregnant a second time. She confided in her mother, who only waved her hands and said, "You live like a queen on that family estate. You'll just have to work it out!" Van beat Monica again and made fun of her fat belly. He never referred to the baby growing within her as their child. This time, she carried the baby to term. When their daughter was two years old, Van tied Monica down and raped her. She became pregnant again, this time with a son.

When Monica's little boy turned three years old, they had a summer pool party at their estate to celebrate his birthday. Her eyes wide with terror, Monica told me how Van joined her in the pool and held her under the water—he wasn't letting her breathe. No one seemed to notice, though, except the three-year-old boy, who jumped in the pool and started hitting his father in protest. Somehow, Monica managed to emerge from the water, gasping for air. Later that night, after everyone had left, Van started abusing his three-year-old boy as punishment for saving his mother. Fearing for her children's lives, Monica took her son and daughter and ran away in such haste that she had no time to dress herself. When she arrived at her parents' house wearing nothing but underwear, her mother finally believed her story. Eventually, Monica braved the previously feared shame of divorce and left Van for good. Today, she is happily remarried. Because she understood the importance of *staying out* once she *got out*, she was able to begin a new life with a good man.

The Risks of Pregnancy

Sadly, many wives and girlfriends who become pregnant die at the hands of their partners—the very people responsible for getting them pregnant. In 2004, Donna St. George, a writer for the *Washington Post*, published her findings from a yearlong investigation that documented 1,327 maternal homicides in the previous fourteen years, or about 295 a year.[38] The data is incomplete due to the fact that many states do not track this type of death, but even so, there is a definite link between pregnancy and homicide. This recently emerging trend seems to be on the rise, too. In 2005, in the State of Maryland, for example, 11 percent of maternal deaths were the result of murder.[39] That means that more mothers die from homicide there than from cardiovascular disorders, embolisms, and accidents. And there is no "typical" victim. She can be of any childbearing age and come from any socioeconomic level. Maryland health researchers Isabelle Horon and Diana Cheng did not expect to find murder to be a leading cause of deaths among pregnant women in their state. "It was a huge surprise," Horon said, quoted in St. George's article. Each state has its own alarming statistics.

---

[38] Donna St. George, "Many New or Expectant Mothers Die Violent Deaths," *The Washington Post* (19 December 2004): A01.

[39] 2007 Annual Report, Maternal Mortality Review Program, Maryland Department of Health and Mental Hygiene, Family Health Administration, & Center for Maternal and Child Health.

Jenny's Story

Jenny's abuse took a different form. Jenny's husband used manipulation to alienate her from all of her friends. "Before I married Alex, I had a full social life. Most of my friends I'd had since childhood," Jenny said. "One by one, I saw less and less of them. My ex-husband's favorite line was, 'You should hear how your friends talk about you behind your back.' He'd often say things like, 'You really don't need them, anyhow; it's just you and me, babe.' He criticized all of my friends, too. After a while, I realized that it wasn't what they were saying, but what he was saying *to* them about *me*. Much later, after the divorce, I felt like I'd come home when I was able to 'find' my friends again."

Post-Traumatic Stress Disorder

After you have gone through the traumas of domestic violence, you are usually filled with fear and anxiety that endure long after the abuse has stopped. This aftershock is a psychological reaction known as post-traumatic stress disorder. In the throes of post-traumatic stress disorder, you don't feel like yourself. Certain sights, smells, and sounds may cause flashbacks to the abuse, calling up memories that trigger the same terror you experienced from the abuse. You may have frequent nightmares and feel irritable and impatient. These are common complaints of someone who has lived through abuse.

Karen Spruill's life was changed by working with victims at a domestic violence shelter in Pennsylvania, and she took their stories with her when she moved to Michigan, where she became involved with an abuse task force. Now living in Orlando, Florida, Spruill co-leads a lay support group, Women in Need of Safety (WINGS) with Sandy, a survivor of domestic violence. WINGS provides a place of prayer and spiritual renewal for victims and survivors of domestic abuse. Among the participants who have suffered the most abuse are church pastors' wives. When women suffer abuse by men who claim to represent God, the emotional and physical damage can be even more intense, for these men often feel justified by God in doling out painful chastisement to their "disobedient" wives who "refuse to submit." Spruill recommends books about emotional healing by pioneer researcher Patricia Evans, *Controlling People* in particular. She also suggests *The Betrayal Bond* by Patrick J. Carnes.

Marsha's Story

When Marsha was in her fifties, the emotional abuse that had typified her thirty-year marriage escalated into physical violence. She didn't linger but left her husband and started nursing school. The worst part of Marsha's abuse was her realization that she had lost her identity. When Marsha had first married Mark, she'd been confident and successful. She'd had many loving friends and family members with whom she'd enjoyed spending time, and she believed that her marital union would only add joy and companionship to her happiness. Bit by bit, however, Mark chipped away at her spirit. He criticized her constantly. But it took years for Marsha to realize what had happened to her. By then, her confidence had been eroded almost entirely, and she couldn't imagine trying to make it on her own. She couldn't understand what had happened to her, and she was stuck in her fear. Her identity seemed to be inextricably wrapped up in her husband's, who seemed to delight in her emotional dependency on him. A severe beating and the ensuing shame finally brought Marsha to her moment of truth. She thought, *I must get out*—and she did!

In her book *The Gaslight Effect*, Dr. Robin Stern exposes the manipulative tactics that other people use to control your life by causing you to doubt yourself. She explains that the relationship involves a "gaslighter"—one who needs to be right in order to preserve his or her own sense of self—and a "gaslightee"—one who allows his or her sense of reality to be defined by the gaslighter in order to preserve that person's approval. The 1944 film *Gaslight* deals with this issue of mind games and actually coined the phrase for this effect. In the film, Gregory (Charles Boyer) attempts to make his wife, Paula (Ingrid Bergman), doubt her own sanity in hopes that she will die and leave him a considerable inheritance. He moves things around in the house, then denies doing it, tells Paula she is frail and ailing, and rigs the gas line to their home so that the lights dim for no apparent reason. Of course, he tells her she's the only one who notices an anomaly in their brightness. While the term "gaslight syndrome" springs from a specific tactic, the manipulative devices and psychological ploys used by gaslighters come in countless forms. If you frequently question your sanity or second-guess your decisions, it is worth considering whether you are a victim of gaslighting.

Red Flags

- You feel as if you are always off balance in the relationship.

- You frequently doubt yourself.

- You ask yourself questions such as *Am I as hypersensitive and demanding as he says I am?*

- You make excuses for his behavior to his family and friends.

Robin Stern gives the following advice:

- **Try to deflect power struggles.** If the fight is heating up, tell him, "I'm very uncomfortable; we'll have to talk about this later." During a heated argument, it's difficult to remember everything that is said and done.

- **Be a reporter.** Keep a well-hidden journal that describes what actually happened in detail. If you're not careful, his view of reality will become yours; the journal will serve as your reality meter, reminding you of what truly transpired.

- **Be willing to leave the relationship.** Susan Heitler, Ph.D., author of *The Power of Two: Secrets to a Strong and Loving Marriage*, suggests making a list of everything he has said or done that really stung, then returning often to the list and reviewing it. A manipulative person will accuse others of behaviors that are actually his own, and if you notice this trend on your list, simply being aware that he is indeed manipulative will help you to free yourself and move on.

Marsha has begun a new life. She focuses on her future and watches for red flags in new relationships. Now that she has her life back, these lines from *Gaslight* seem particularly relevant to her. Paula laments, "It has been a long night." Her friend, Cameron, reassures her: "But it will end. It's starting to clear. In the morning when the sun rises, sometimes it's hard to believe there ever was a night."

5
"I'M A WRECK AT WORK"

ॐ

Domestic violence does not stay at home when its victims go to work. Signs and symptoms of domestic violence often follow an abused woman into her workplace and invade not only her office but also those around it. Domestic violence affects productivity and raises the risk of violence in the workplace. A woman who is being abused at home often arrives consistently late to work, using a different excuse for her tardiness every time. She may appear shaky, distracted, nervous, anxious, confused, depressed, and even tearful. She may avoid coworkers because she doesn't want to admit or talk about "it." Her hands may tremble frequently. The quality of her work usually diminishes. Often, increased absenteeism and escalated medical expenses will follow.

> ॐ
>
> Domestic violence affects productivity and raises the risk of violence in the workplace.

Domestic violence costs employers hundreds of millions of dollars each year due to abused employees' increased medical expenses.[40] Decreased productivity due to domestic violence causes a loss of nearly $727.8 million per year with more than 7.9 million paid

---

[40] Pennsylvania Blue Shield Institute, *Social Problems and Rising Health Care Costs in Pennsylvania* (1992): 3–5.

workdays lost each year.[41] In one case, a wrongful death action suit against an employer who failed to respond to an employee's risk of domestic violence on the job cost the employer $850,000.[42]

The cost of intimate partner violence exceeds $5.8 billion each year, $4.1 billion of which covers direct medical and mental health care services.[43] A large portion of this $4.1 billion is paid for by employers.[44] Employers are aware of this economic burden: 44 percent of executives surveyed said that domestic violence increases their health care costs.[45] With one in four American women reporting abuse by a husband or boyfriend at some point in her life, it is certain that at least one employee in every mid- to large-sized company is affected by domestic violence.

How can coworkers or supervisors help an employee whom they suspect may be a victim of domestic abuse?

Try to address the subject gently and discreetly. Allow the employee to engage in dialogue by asking her open-ended questions. Because of today's legal and privacy climate, it is crucial to assure confidentiality. Provide her with the phone number for the National Domestic Violence Hotline (1-800-799-SAFE).

If you are a concerned coworker:

- Watch your coworkers vigilantly for possible signs of domestic violence, such as changes in behavior and work performance, lack of concentration, increased or unexplained absences, the placing or receiving of harassing phone calls, and the

---

[41] *Costs of Intimate Partner Violence against Women in the United States, 2003.* Centers for Disease Control and Prevention, National Center for Injury Prevention and Control. Atlanta, GA.

[42] D. F. Burke, "When Employees Are Vulnerable, Employers Are Too." *The National Law Journal* (January 2000).

[43] *Costs of Intimate Partner Violence against Women in the United States, 2003.* Centers for Disease Control and Prevention, National Centers for Injury Prevention and Control. Atlanta, GA.

[44] *Facts on the Workplace and Domestic Violence*, Family Violence Prevention Fund.

[45] Pennsylvania Blue Shield Institute, *Social Problems and Rising Health Care Costs in Pennsylvania* (1992): 3–5.

appearance of bruises or injuries that are unexplained or that generate explanations that just don't seem to add up.

- If a coworker confides in you that she is being abused, believe her.

- Listen without judging. As we discussed earlier, victims of abuse often begin believing their abusers' negative messages and feel responsible, ashamed, and fearful of judgment.

- Tell her that she does not have to stay in the abusive situation. Let her know that help is available and easily accessible.

- Call the company's employee assistance program or a local domestic violence program to receive confidential advice and resources.

If you are a victim:

- Talk with someone whom you trust, such as your supervisor, human resources manager, or employee assistance counselor.

- If your company has its own security department, notify them of your safety concerns. Consider providing security, your supervisors, and anyone working in the reception area with a picture of your abuser and a copy of the protective orders against him.

- Arrange to have your telephone calls screened. Harassing calls should be transferred to security's extension. You might also consider having your name and extension number removed from the automatic telephone directory.

- Review the safety of your parking arrangement. Have a member of security personnel escort you to your car after work. Obtain a parking space near the building entrance to minimize the amount of time you spend in the parking lot.

- Ask coworkers to call the police if your partner threatens or harasses you while you are at work.

- Inquire about flexible or alternate work hours.

- Ask to relocate your workspace to a more secure area.

- Review the safety of your childcare arrangements. Provide your children's daycare provider with a photo of your abuser and a copy of your protective order against him. If it seems advisable, consider selecting a new daycare site.

- Notify your supervisor or manager of the situation and the possible need to be absent. Supervisors/managers cannot offer assistance until an employee self-discloses.

- Discuss the options available to you with your supervisor and human resources manager. Involve your local employee counselor, if necessary. The counselor can assist you with developing a safety plan.

> ৯
>
> Establish clear-cut policies to ensure that any employees seeking help for domestic abuse will find support at their workplace.

What can your company or organization do to help? Every company should take initiative to promote awareness and provide education about domestic violence and its far-reaching scope. Employers should not be afraid to address the issue openly. If they remain silent and pretend that the problem doesn't exist, it will remain one of the best-kept secrets in America. Until we bring it out and discuss it, this tragedy will continue to tear apart individuals and families. Your organization needs to establish clear-cut policies to ensure that any employees seeking help for domestic abuse will find support at their workplace. If a company sustains silence about the issue, this will only reinforce the feelings of shame and fear that victims attach in their minds to the abuse they suffer, and they will remain silent rather than seek help.

Countless companies across the country are starting to recognize that responding to domestic violence is "good business." The following checklist is a resource for employers to use in order to address domestic violence in their workplaces.

- Join your company's response with a larger, community-wide response. For example, you may choose to participate in lobbying efforts to enact domestic violence legislation.

- Organize training seminars to educate your employees about recognizing the signs and symptoms of domestic abuse. Establish workplace policies regarding domestic violence and discuss them with staff members to promote understanding and awareness.

- Offer counseling to employees and make them aware of the services provided by your employee assistance program and/ or local domestic violence programs.

- Write or commission informative articles about domestic violence to be published in your company newsletter and in local newspapers. Create or order posters, brochures, or other print media with messages against domestic violence and display them around the workplace.

- Follow any measures that will improve the security of your employees. Something as simple as providing security personnel with the photograph of a batterer can save a life.

- Select a staff member to serve as the primary contact person for all matters related to domestic violence. Make sure that this individual is trained in dealing with domestic violence and has great compassion and concern for its victims.

The Value of Contribution

If we want to stop the cycle of abuse, we need to be a part of the solution. Everyone has something helpful to contribute. Staff writer Tony Natale of Phoenix, Arizona, shed light on domestic violence in the workplace when he wrote and published Jennifer's story in the *East Valley Tribune*.[46] Jennifer was a middle-management employee whose ex-fiancé had begun to harass her at work. His behavior became that of a stalker, and Jennifer's coworkers were increasingly alarmed. Jennifer was eventually fired, but the company still denied the problem of work-related domestic violence and its extensive scope. It is critical that domestic violence be addressed in the workplace. It is equally important to foster a corporate culture that encourages employees to discuss domestic violence openly.

A primary source for this article was Stephanie Angelo, an experienced human resource employee who founded Human Resource Essential, a company based in Tempe, Arizona, that specializes in domestic violence issues in the workplace. Her primary aim is to work with companies' human resources departments to establish programs to handle domestic abuse affecting employees. Many companies make the mistake of keeping their distance, not wanting to get involved in their employees' personal lives and problems. It is Angelo's mission to reverse this attitude among employers.

Angelo's first meeting with each new client is largely instructional: she teaches managers how to identify victims of domestic abuse. Then, she presents ways in which they should speak with an employee about the abuse he or she is suffering. These managers are trained to direct the employee to a professional counselor, for skilled people alone should give advice to victims.

Angelo also manages the Web site kidzweyes.com, which she created to provide parents and children with information about safety programs for young people. In addition to this Web site, you can visit www.endabuse.org, established by the Family Violence Prevention Fund, to access pertinent information.

Angelo's firm is following a national trend among companies that are trying harder to solve a major problem.

Two companies that "get it" are Liz Claiborne, Inc., and Macy's, Inc. In 1991, Liz Claiborne, Inc., invested more than $7 million in

---

[46] Tony Natale, "Tempe Woman Shines Light on Domestic Abuse." *The East Valley Tribune* (3 April 2005).

its Love Is Not Abuse campaign. Three years ago, company executives updated their domestic violence policy and implemented a new program, "Safe Place in the Workplace," to train human resources, legal, security, and management personnel to recognize and address the issue.

Macy's, Inc., sponsors workshops to heighten awareness of domestic violence issues among employees, according to Gail Nutt, Senior Vice President of Community Affairs and Diversity Management. Special company procedures let employees know that it is safe for them to come forward with any domestic violence issues they may be experiencing. Both large and small businesses can do *good* business by conducting seminars about domestic violence in the workplace and working to increase awareness about the magnitude of this issue.

Amanda's Story

For Amanda, her job was her sanity— the hours she spent at work were her sole respite from the abuse she suffered at home. Work was her escape. As a flight attendant for a major airline, she could leave town for days at a time and "recuperate" from the abuse.

Bill and Amanda married when both were in their forties. They each entered the marriage with a good job and a quality income—they lived well. But only after they married did Amanda discover Bill's dark side. She admitted to overlooking and ignoring dangerous clues during their courtship that should have signaled red flags for her. Instead, she maintained her belief that Bill had the potential to be a loving partner, and she accepted his marriage proposal.

> ❧
> Only after they married did Amanda discover Bill's dark side.

Amanda described Bill as a flashy, handsome man. He came from a prominent Hollywood family, and while many people viewed him as arrogant, none would have suspected him to be capable of ruthless violence against his wife.

The abuse was subtle at first. Bill used manipulative and controlling tactics with Amanda, but her frequent travels as a flight attendant broke the cycle enough to render it unnoticeable. She would return to a man who put her on a pedestal, which further mitigated the impact of his manipulation. One red flag emerged shortly after their marriage, when Amanda's beloved animals disappeared—never to be found again. Amanda later learned that Bill had killed them. Slowly but surely, Bill picked away at Amanda's life and identity until he had stolen them completely. The mental and emotional manipulation escalated to physical abuse. One time, Bill pounded on her head so severely that she had to be rushed to the hospital. Bill took her to the emergency room, where he even admitted his responsibility for her injuries: a brain concussion and loss of vision, which would last one month. The police asked Amanda if she wanted to press charges against him, but she declined, knowing that without the ability to see, she would require Bill's help. She absolved him because she had no one else to take care of her.

When Amanda's friends and coworkers found out about her condition, she crafted a fictitious excuse, saying that she had been in an automobile accident, the force of which had propelled her through her car's windshield. In order to resume work as a flight attendant, though, she had to undergo an examination by the medical department. When she lied again about what had happened to cause her injuries, the doctor told her, "Amanda, we know the truth." She didn't know that the hospital where she had been treated was required by law to report to her employer what had happened. The airline had known all along.

Another major blow to Amanda was the loss of her financial security. The IRS sent her a notice that their income tax refund was going to be appropriated as payment for the college loan debts Bill still owed to the government. Bill was also a chronic gambler. It didn't take long for Amanda to realize that he was going to bankrupt them. She knew then that she had to file for divorce. When Bill's family learned of Amanda's intentions, they turned their backs on her. She never heard from them again, in spite of repeated attempts on her part to contact them.

The airline that employed Amanda offered leadership training for professional flight attendants. She enrolled in this program, which she credits with providing a crossroads of change in her life. It inspired her with an idea of what she wanted to do with the rest of her life. As a fifty-year-old, Amanda made a list of personal goals, which included creating an escape and safety plan. Amanda no longer has nightmares. She is happily remarried and enjoying a productive career.

Safety Tips

- A tip from tae kwon do: the elbow is the strongest point on your body. If you are close enough to an attacker to use it, do!

- Keep a hidden financial stash. You can be safe only with credit cards and cash on hand.

- Keep copies of your most important papers—the titles to your car and home, your birth certificate and those of your children, important financial documents—in a safe but easily accessible place.

- Contrary to what the health experts say, you should always take the *elevator* instead of the stairs. A stairwell is a horrible place to be alone because it offers enough concealment to make a perfect crime spot. This is especially true at night! Also, many elevators are monitored from within and without by closed-circuit cameras. Knowing that he is being recorded may deter an abuser from harming you.

- When your car is parked in a garage or lot:

  A. Be aware of your surroundings as you approach your car. When you reach your car, look inside at the passenger side floor and backseat, and look under your car, too.

B. If you are parked to the right of a large van, especially if it's unmarked, enter your car from the passenger-side door. Many abusers attack their victims by pulling them into their vans while the women are attempting to get into their cars.

C. Look at the cars parked on either side of your vehicle. If your stalker is sitting in the car next to yours, you should return immediately to the mall, church, office, school, or other building and find someone—preferably a security officer—to escort you to your vehicle. It is always better to be safe than sorry, and better paranoid than dead.

- If you are out shopping, working, dining, or doing another activity and your abuser has been stalking you, do not sit idly in your car afterward. Your abuser is probably still watching you, and if you delay your departure, it gives him the perfect opportunity to enter your car on the passenger side, put a gun to your head or threaten you in some other way, and direct you where to drive. As soon as you get into your car, you should lock the doors and leave immediately.

- Women are sometimes ensnared by their sympathy. You can be kind and considerate, but be cautious so that your kindness doesn't get you raped or killed. Serial killer Ted Bundy was a good-looking, well-educated man who always played on the sympathies of unsuspecting women. He would limp, walk with a cane, wear a fake arm cast, or feign other physical difficulty, then ask a woman for help carrying something heavy to his car. This was the prelude to abduction—and murder. More than thirty women were assaulted and killed by Ted Bundy, mostly because they took pity on him.

- One of the most creative cons is the crying baby scam. One woman heard a baby's cries coming from her front porch, but before opening the door, she wisely called the police. The operator told her, "Whatever you do, do not open the door!" He then told her about the latest con, which involves using the recording of a baby's cry to coax concerned women out of their homes and into the trap of a waylaying abductor. Do not open your door if you hear a baby crying. This scam was mentioned on *America's Most Wanted.*

Pass this information on to other women who may need to be reminded that it's better to be safe than sorry. This information may save a life.

Robin's Story

"I would leave Bill, and he would find me. This cycle repeated itself over and over," said Robin. "Eventually, he wore me down. Then, I would acquiesce. He'd find me again. I was moving every six months. I lived with the fear of his continual stalking. It was terrifying. I realized that there was only one way he would leave me alone. He would kill me or kill himself."

Even though Bill and Robin had gotten a divorce, Bill constantly accused Robin of adulterous affairs. If there was any man around—a plumber, a groundskeeper, a male neighbor—Bill was sure that Robin was having an affair with him. In fact, a paranoid jealousy of Robin's twenty-five-year-old next-door neighbor drove Bill, who was a weightlifter and bodybuilder, to beat the man with a two-by-four. His intent was to kill him. When Bill thought that he had succeeded, he went next door and broke into Robin's condo. Robin was in the pantry and didn't hear him enter. He approached her silently from behind, put his hands around her neck, and began to strangle her. Petite and delicate, Robin was no match for her husband's strength, and she thought that her life was over. All of a sudden, she heard an unfamiliar male voice urge loudly, "Fight back! Stall for time!" Robin believed that the voice was a form of divine intervention, and she obediently began fighting back. Bill was unable to cut off her airway as she thrashed about, focusing on the voice and its message. When Bill attempted to rape her, she did not resist him—she was stalling for time, just as the voice said that she should do. Those few minutes of agony would save Robin's life.

Before Bill could do anything else to her, the front door flew open to reveal a squad of police officers standing there. Robin was numb with disbelief at the police officers' presence, for she had been unable to summon them. She later learned that the neighbor whom Bill had beaten with the two-by-four had regained consciousness and called the police. He had given them his address, oblivious to what was going on next door, but the police officers arrived at Robin's house by mistake! They questioned Robin, who was in shock, and she told them that she was fine. They asked her why she had blood running down her forehead. Bill was arrested, jailed, and eventually incarcerated for thirty years. The Nevada legal system worked for Robin. But even after Bill was behind bars, the district attorney told her that she must move to preserve her own safety.

Robin said that it took her a year to calm down. She feels safe for now, but the knowledge that Bill will be eligible for parole in fifteen years is a nagging discomfort. Even so, Robin has a renewed appreciation for freedom. She finally feels that her life has a sense of order, and she even hopes to remarry someday.

Joan's Story

There was no denying that Joan suffered abuse. The former model's coworkers saw her sizeable bruises and black eyes. They constantly worried about her, but they couldn't get her to open up about what was going on at home. Joan always came up with excuses for what had happened, trying to hide the deeds of her husband, Dan, who was wild with jealousy. He constantly accused her of having affairs. One evening, Joan had gone to a Tupperware party with her friend, Lora, and the two stopped for coffee on the way home. They had been talking for some time when Joan said suddenly, "I'd better get going. Dan doesn't like for me to be out after ten o'clock." When Joan arrived at home, her illuminated watch read two minutes past ten as she walked up the dark front porch steps. She unlocked the door and was proceeding through the entryway when a fist smashed her face with such force that it knocked her backwards onto the porch. Then, Dan dragged her into the house and beat her face repeatedly. "That will teach you!" He shouted. "I saw you sitting by that guy in McDonald's—yeah! Some Tupperware party!"

Joan was bleeding so profusely that she started to choke on the blood. Even Dan was scared. He drove her to the hospital and dropped her off at the emergency room, then took off. Joan fainted just outside the hospital entrance. It took three surgeries to repair her face, but her appearance was forever changed. Her friend Lora said, "When I went to the hospital the next day to see Joan, I didn't recognize her. In fact, I still don't recognize her. She just doesn't look the same anymore."

After this violent episode, Joan moved in with her parents. She didn't press charges against Dan, but she did file for divorce. Dan sent gifts and floral bouquets to her at the hospital during her recovery period. He tried to pursue reconciliation further by showering her with gifts and love letters at her workplace. But Joan was terrified of him. When his gifts were delivered to her office, they always caused an emotional tailspin. She would run to the restroom and vomit.

Several years later, Dan had remarried, and Joan heard that he was beating his new wife. Joan said that she regrets not having pressed any charges. But Dan is serving time, thanks to his new wife, who did press charges. Joan has never remarried; she says that she never will. Nightmares plague her, and she will "never, ever, be the same," she said.

Amanda's Story

Amanda developed a unique analogy to express how she felt about the abuse she endured for three years. "Have you ever tried to prepare a pomegranate?" she asked me. "Especially at Christmastime, I like to make recipes using pomegranates. This fruit has to be torn apart and pried open to access the seeds. That's how I felt—pried open like a pomegranate!"

Shortly after Amanda and Mike were married, Amanda started a job as a receptionist at an advertising firm. Later on, she was promoted and became an assistant of public relations. Thus began the abuse. "I was not allowed to have any social life without Mike," Amanda said. "There were no more girls' nights out. Whenever I did go out with friends or coworkers, I'd see Mike at another table at the same restaurant. He would even go to the same movie theaters and grocery stores. It was weird."

Mike's odd behavior created awkward situations with Amanda's coworkers and made them uncomfortable. One of her friends told her, "You'd better take Mike to see a shrink." She could tell that something was wrong with him.

Mike would not stop spying, though, so to keep her friends from feeling uncomfortable, Amanda started coming up with excuses to stay home rather than go out with them. They called her less and less often, and if they happened to call while she was not home, Mike would never deliver their messages.

Mike's possessive behavior started affecting Amanda's career, as well. "When I got promoted to public relations, I was required to attend social functions. He'd show up drunk and yank me out of the event," Amanda said. "The first time it happened, I apologized to my boss. I remember shaking as I lied to him. I told him that Mike was on medicine that affected him emotionally. The second time it happened, my boss called me in and told me that he'd have to re-place me because of Mike's behavior. I went home and told Mike. He responded, 'You'd better find another job; we have bills to pay.' Then, he fell asleep watching television."

Amanda promptly packed her suitcase and left. She was never tempted to go back. Fortunately, her boss rehired her six months later.

Liz's Story

Family members, friends, and coworkers had been begging Liz to leave her husband. Her coworkers were especially worried by her frequent absences due to a variety of "illnesses." Liz had become so thin that she was starting to look anorexic. Finally, she decided that she and her two children couldn't take it anymore. After fifteen years of a harrowing marriage, she filed for divorce.

Even after the divorce, Liz's ex-husband continued harassing her at work. Now, her coworkers feared for her life and urged her to relocate out of town. But Liz liked her job, and she lived in a large metropolitan city that she deemed plenty big for her ex-husband and herself. She valued her coworkers' concern, though, so she moved to another part of town, bought a new car, requested an unlisted telephone number, and enrolled her two teenaged children in a different high school. Even with all of these precautions, however, Liz was not safe.

Her ex-husband discovered where she was living and ambushed her and the children. In a matter of minutes, he shot and killed them all before turning the gun on himself. Liz's coworkers were aghast. "What if he'd come to the office?" they wondered. "Could we have helped, or would he have killed us, too?"

Following this tragedy, the local sheriff's office reported that it receives between twenty-five and thirty-five phone calls reporting domestic violence every day. That particular county has a unit with four detectives assigned to domestic violence cases. Their advice is the following: "The first time you feel intimidated by a partner, get help and reach out. Don't be ashamed. Nothing is worth losing your life over."

> ❧
> Don't be ashamed. Nothing is worth losing your life over.

6

"His Ugly Words Broke My Spirit"

かん

There once was a little boy who had a bad temper. His father gave him a bag full of nails and told him that every time he lost his temper, he would have to hammer a nail into the back of the wooden fence that surrounded their yard.

At the end of the first day, the boy had driven thirty-seven nails into the fence.

Over the next few weeks, as he learned to control his anger, the number of nails he hammered dwindled daily.

He soon discovered that holding his temper was easier than driving nails into the fence.

The day finally came when the boy did not lose his temper at all.

He told his father, who suggested that he start pulling out one nail for every day that he was able to control his temper.

Days passed until finally the young boy was able to tell his father that every last nail had been pulled from the fence.

His father took him by the hand and led him to the fence.

He said, "You have done well, my son. But look at the holes in the fence. This fence will never be the same. When you say things in *anger, they leave scars just like these holes left by the nails. You can put a knife in a man and draw it out, and regardless of how many times you say, 'I'm sorry,' the wound will still be there."*

—Author Anonymous

If you were not raised in a controlling family, you may not appreciate the potent dynamics of power and control. Words can be powerful weapons of control.

Emotional Manipulation

> ❧
> Perhaps the most powerful strategy of controlling other people is emotional manipulation.

In his book *Breaking Controlling Powers*, Roberts Liardon describes the many faces of control. Perhaps the most powerful strategy of controlling other people is emotional manipulation. Tears, rage, and silence—these are a few examples of emotive charades that can be conjured in an attempt to get one's own way by sending the other person on a guilt trip. Silence, which is a form of rejection, is an especially powerful form of emotional manipulation.

Many people are at the mercy of their own emotions, which seem to wield incredible control over their thoughts, words, and actions. They tend to make decisions based on feelings rather than on rational thought, which explains why they make so many wrong or misguided decisions. Many people are propelled into marriage by "a feeling," only to find out that they've made a terrible mistake. Businesspeople who conduct deals based on feelings may lose everything for which they bargained, especially if they felt someone to be trustworthy who turned on them, took the money, and ran, so to speak.

If you disagree with someone who uses emotional manipulation, he or she may say, "You don't love me anymore!" What should you say at that point? Try saying, "Well, I don't like it when you act like this, and I don't have to agree with you." Phrases such as "You don't love me anymore" are subtle forms of manipulation.

If tears won't work, a controlling person may resort to anger. Most people have trouble knowing how to handle someone who is angry. What is the best thing to do? Stay calm. Look at the person, state the truth, and then walk out. Leave the person alone with his rage.

If anger has not proven effective, controlling people will usually employ another weapon: silence. They shut you out and ignore anything you may say or do, which keeps you dangling and leaves you wondering. Those who are most susceptible to this type of control are individuals with a weak sense of self or low self-esteem. Because they derive their identities largely from those with whom they regularly converse, they can't stand it when these people are nonresponsive. Desperate to draw their controllers out of their strategic, tight-lipped states, the victims of this type of control will do or say whatever their controllers desire. People who worry about what others think of them will miss the truth they need to hear. It is important not to be overly dependent on other people and their opinions of you. If you are a dependent person, you can't enjoy normal fellowship with others because your joy, happiness, and thoughts are not your own, and you will be an easy victim of emotional control.

Spiritual Manipulation

It is sad but true: some pastors, ministers, and other clergymen can contribute to an abused person's confusion rather than helping him or her to escape the abuse. If a pastor knows about the abuse yet believes it to be justified, he may join the abuser in blaming the victim and thereby perpetuate the problem. Janet was being abused by her husband, but when she confided in her pastor, he told her that she "must have sinned," which he considered a reasonable explanation for her husband's abuse. If Janet had been a "good girl" and a submissive wife, her husband would not have had reason to abuse. The idea that husbands are responsible for physically punishing

> ❦
> The idea that
> husbands are
> responsible
> for physically
> punishing
> their wives'
> wrongdoings
> and "sins" is
> fallacious.

their wives' wrongdoings and "sins" is fallacious. Pastors and other church leaders must correct this erroneous thinking, if it exists in their congregations, and should offer support and assistance, not guilt and condemnation, to victims seeking help.

Words of Failure and Defeat, Unnatural Obligation, Guilt, Criticism, and Intimidation

Many people do not realize how profoundly they are affected by the words of others, especially words of failure and defeat. Even body language can be intimidating. A certain look or the lifting of an eyebrow can make a strong statement. Someone may noticeably skirt a specific topic of conversation in order to control another person by allowing no opportunity for discussion.

Are you being controlled? Realize that as long as someone is controlling you, he or she will never permit you to reach your highest potential. The greatest problem for people who are controlled is not the control itself, but rather the need to acknowledge that they are being controlled. What are some likely indications that you are under the control of someone else?

If you feel physically tired and drained of energy all of the time, this may indicate the physical results of psychological abuse. Compelling research has correlated mental abuse with physical problems and illnesses. In her article "Psychological Abuse = Physical Abuse," published in 2002 by *Web MD Health News*, Jeanie Lerche Davis wrote about a large-scale study performed by Dr. Ann L. Coker and colleagues at the University of Texas School of Public Health and colleagues. Examining data collected by the National Violence against Women Survey, a random phone survey that canvassed about 8,000 men and 8,000 women across the United States, Coker and her colleagues found that of the respondents, nearly one-third of women and one-fourth of men reported experiencing some form of abuse sometime in their lives. The most frequent form reported was psychological abuse, which the researchers had defined as "verbal abuse and abuse of power of control," according to Coker. Whether the abuse they suffered was psychological or physical, the victims reported significantly poorer health—both mental and physical—than respondents who had not been abused. The study showed that women who are psychologically or physically abused are more likely to have such physiological effects as depression, drug use, chronic disease, chronic mental illness, and physical injuries, Davis said.

Another indication that you are under someone's control is if you find that you feel content until the controller sets off a controlling signal to you, whether with words or nonverbal communication. Controlling signals that you are able to recognize should be bright red flags. These signals may cause you to become suddenly exhausted, confused, or imbalanced. Make a careful evaluation of your relationships, even those with members of your own family. If a friendship is not edifying and encouraging to you, deal with the problem by discussing it with the other person. If he or she refuses to amend the issue, leave the relationship. Don't worry about hurt feelings—you will only experience more hurt if you stay, and it's unlikely that he or she feels the same sense of guilt that you do.

If you feel compelled to check with someone and obtain his or her permission before doing anything, you are probably being controlled. It's one thing to tell your supervisor where you are or to let your family members know what time you expect to be home—that's common courtesy. When your spouse or parents want to know where you're going, their interest is due to their natural love and concern for you. They are not trying to control you. But if you feel as if you're reporting to your prison warden when you tell someone about your plans and whereabouts, it's another thing altogether. Altogether wrong.

If you feel lost in a sea of depression and listlessness most of the time, it is likely because you are being controlled. Controlling people will interfere with your goals, foil your plans, and rob your passion for life. They will also steal your vision and replace it with their own, which is unlikely to generate the same enthusiasm and will cause you to feel defeated.

If you're having fun with your friends and suddenly lose all your joy when a certain person enters the room, that person is controlling you. A controlling spouse or partner will be jealous and possessive of you. He will feel threatened when you as much as talk to someone other than he, and he will do everything he can to isolate you from everyone else so he can have you all to himself.

A controlling person controls another through fear, abuse, domination, and underhanded manipulation. He or she dominates and destroys the other's joy and sense of adventure. If you are to break free from the domination of others, you will need to know how to distinguish between normal, loving concern and unnatural, obsessive control.

What Causes a Person to Become a Controller?

- **Hurts and wounds, especially from childhood.** The emotionally or physically wounded child promises himself, *I'll never get hurt like that again.* To fulfill this promise, it is necessary for him to control his entire world, including those around him. He constructs a thick wall around his innermost self to shut out the whole world.

- **Growing up in a controlling environment.** Some people were raised in households where the atmosphere was heavy with control and manipulation. They were brought up by controlling parents who passed along their techniques and tactics to their children, who grow up and mirror the same behaviors.

- **The need to feel powerful and confident.** Controlling other people boosts controllers' self-esteem and makes them feel comfortable. They want other people to serve them and follow their directions. It makes them feel superior.

What about Control by the Opposite Sex?

Most dating men want sex. Usually, dating women simply want to be loved. Men may speak romantic words and clever witticisms, but only because they think—often correctly—that these tactics will lead to sex. Many women confuse sex with love, so they acquiesce to have sex in order to get what they think will be "love." It's an age-old story that will probably continue for ages. Many men control women with such phrases as "I love you," and "If you loved me, you would…." They speak these falsehoods to get women to fall for them and to give them what they desire most: sex. Women who blindly believe these professions and rush into sex are permitting themselves to be controlled. Many teenaged girls have fallen for these lines and compromised their virginity at a young age. The result is often a compromised youth, as many will become pregnant and spend much of their adolescence as mothers.

Another characteristic of a controller is that he accuses you of the things he himself does. This often happens in marriages, especially when a battered wife begins to break free, at least emotionally, from a controlling husband. To induce her to stay, the husband will accuse her of neglecting her household duties. Meanwhile, *he's* the one who is neglecting the duties of a loving husband; the wife is actually still doing her part. Control is a vicious cycle propelled by manipulation of many kinds.

Are You a Controller?

You may be a controller if:

- You think that you will feel important or be accepted only if you issue orders and give commands to others, making sure that they do things your way.

- You feel possessive of someone (or several people). You insist that you know what's best for the other person, and you reject his or her judgment and decision-making ability. You often belittle the person's choices and point out his or her flaws.

- You don't allow anyone to voice opinions or ideas that differ from yours. Your mind is set against discussing contrary views, let alone accepting them. If someone manages to voice a different opinion, you simply ignore him and keep doing your own thing.

- You are jealous of the attention and affections of someone and you feel threatened each time this person makes a new acquaintance or forges a new friendship.

- You feel overprotective of someone and determine to protect him or her from every experience, good or bad. You attack whatever might keep this person from spending time with you and try to rid his or her life of it as quickly as possible. You will go to any lengths and spare no expense to make sure that this person will spend the majority of his or her time with you.

- You singlehandedly make all decisions for your spouse and yourself, including where you both work, where you attend church, how you manage your bank accounts, where you travel for vacation, how you raise your children, and so forth.

- You criticize almost every move made and statement spoken by the other person.

- Your life revolves around nurturing and developing another human being. It may look as if this individual is controlling you, which is possible; however, if your "care and concern" stifle and suffocate this person, if you are living vicariously through this person, and if you use your identity as "caregiver" to justify making every decision in his or her stead, you are probably the one in control.

How Do You Break Free from Control?

If you recognize that another person is controlling you, observe just how he is doing so. Look for patterns and methods of control so that you can understand his tactics and their effects on you.

Once you understand the modus operandi of his control and the ways in which he manipulates your behaviors, identify changes that you can make in your own thought patterns and actions in order to resist his control and oppose his ploys. Then, write them down so that you can refer to them when you wonder how to resist.

For example, if your controller uses the tactic of silence, determine not to respond to his silence. Even if he goes two weeks without speaking to you, do not allow yourself to feel guilty. Go on and enjoy your life—who cares if he's miserable and put out? Remind yourself that his silence is a self-imposed state that he assumed with the intention of controlling you. If you follow through with this plan, silence will no longer be an effective method of controlling you.

Be aware, though, that he may react to your resistance with another tactic, such as stalking. Be prepared and don't hesitate to use your escape plan if you feel threatened. The controlling person may say something like, "If you don't do what I say, I'm going to leave you!" If he does, you should reply, "Good. Do it!" This type of assertive statement will show him that you can go on without him; your independence is more than adequate, and he is not necessary for your happiness or well-being. Nonchalance on your part, even if feigned, will undermine his plan to make you come crawling back to him at the thought of his departure.

Exhibiting your self-sufficiency will frustrate him, and he may become aggressive. Be prepared for this reaction and refuse to be intimidated. You have plenty of people to back you up—friends, family, police, shelter workers, and others. Know, too, that withstanding his pleas and ignoring his threats may make him angry enough to end the relationship. Stand your ground. Once you have gone your separate ways, do not seek reconciliation. If he begs for you to come back and you consent, your situation will probably be worse than it ever was before.

Control Is Also a Spiritual Problem

Realize that control is not just a natural psychological problem—it is also a spiritual problem. Human nature is naturally self-serving and controlling. Think of the two-year-old who throws a tantrum when he can't have his own way. An abuser's urge to control is like that of many "terrible" two-year-olds. The next time you experience unacceptable, controlling behavior, do not feel guilty and try to repair the relationship. Have the courage to separate. God does not want us to align ourselves with heartless, controlling people. If you are able to cut the cord of control in your life, you will be set free.

Biblical Bill of Rights

by Hope for the Heart, a women's shelter

- You have the right to receive respect from your mate.

  "Husbands, in the same way be considerate as you live with your wives, and treat them with respect" (1 Peter 3:7).

- You have the right to a relationship of mutual submission.

  "Submit to one another out of reverence for Christ" (Ephesians 5:21).

- You have the right to speak the truth in a loving way.

  "Speaking the truth of love, we will in all things grow up into him who is the Head, that is, Christ" (Ephesians 4:15).

- You have the right to express anger in an appropriate manner.

  "'In your anger do not sin': Do not let the sun go down while you are still angry" (Ephesians 4:26).

- You have the right to report the abuse to governmental authorities.

  "Submit yourselves for the Lord's sake to every author-ity instituted among men..., who are sent by him to punish those who do wrong and to commend those who do right" (1 Peter 2:13–14).

- You have the right to leave an abusive environment.

  "The prudent see danger and take refuge, but the simple keep going and suffer for it" (Proverbs 27:12).

- You have the right to spend personal time alone.

  "Very early in the morning, while it was still dark, Jesus got up, left the house and went off to a solitary place, where he prayed" (Mark 1:35).

- You have the right to use your unique talents and gifts to serve others.

  "Each one should use whatever gift he has received to serve others, faithfully administering God's grace in its various forms" (1 Peter 4:10).

- You have the right to receive emotional and spiritual support from others.

  "Let us not give up meeting together,...but let us encour-age one another—and all the more as you see the Day ap-proaching" (Hebrews 10:25).

How Do You Confront the Controller?

In confronting a controller about his or her behavior, you must be strong and stand your ground. Refuse to be swayed easily by elo-quent articulation and empty rhetoric, which he or she may use to try to confuse you. You need to say, "You've controlled me in various ways, but these methods of manipulation will no longer work in my life. You must change the way you treat me, or we cannot continue this relationship."

When you make this type of statement, you can expect several typical reactions. He may become defensive and ask such questions as, "Do you mean to tell me that you don't appreciate what I've done for you?" Be careful not to back down from your demands. During the course of this confrontation, you must defer to reason and rational thinking, not emotions and quick sympathies. If your emotions get the best of you, his defensive ploy will probably prompt you to apologize and retract your statement. "Oh, I'm sorry. I was wrong," you'll say. "You have done so much for me." The controller will continue, "You know that I love you, and we have to work this out. No one will ever love you like I do." You'll start to cry, and he will comfort you, enfolding you in his arms—and restoring you to his clutches of control.

If the controlling person is not able to bring you to tears of penitence, he will use anger. He will make threats. He will launch a cyclical attack of jealousy, pride, control, fear, and so forth. Be careful that you don't fall into confusion. Just remind yourself that even the most mercurial of people cannot change emotions so quickly; his insatiable desire to control is causing him to display these fast-changing feelings in an attempt to force you to submit. Be strong and stoic, armed with the knowledge of what is really happening and denying your instinct to compromise.

Know this: you are in a war! If you're timid and have trouble standing up for yourself, you had better round up a few strong friends to support you. After the confrontation, don't regurgitate what just happened. Instead, try to shut your mind off. Go for a walk. Pray. Meditate. If you're not willing to pay the price and confront a controlling person, you will not have a healthy life. Your spiritual and emotional growth will be stunted.

Sandy's Story

Many women can relate to Sandy's experience. She was caught in the cycle of control. Her husband's insidious abuse came on slowly, escaping Sandy's notice until the day that she woke up and had no desire to get out of bed. She felt worse every day but forced herself out of bed, knowing that going to work was her sole escape from her husband. Sandy endured days, weeks, months…and years of abuse. "He constantly verbally demeaned me," Sandy said. "It was character assassination, and finally, my spirit was broken."

Her spirit's destruction was a slow and painful process. Sandy had discovered early on in their marriage that Tom was totally self-absorbed. One evening, when she complained about a hard day at work, he turned on her and said, "I don't want to hear about your problems. I have my own problems. If you need someone to listen to you, talk to the dog."

Another night, Sandy came home from the grocery store, having purchased every item that Tom had written out on a list. When he discovered the single purchase that was not on the list—a box of crackers—he screamed at Sandy. Later that same evening, he summoned her harshly to the bathroom. With a fierce look in his eyes, he demanded, "What's wrong with this picture?" Sandy hadn't the slightest idea what he was referring to. "Can't you see that the trash can is half full?" he then shouted.

Sandy realized that she needed to get out of the marriage. Fortunately, she didn't wait. She knew that verbal abuse was just a precursor to probable escalation into violence. She had the courage to escape from the relationship before Tom's behavior got out of control.

Another book by Patricia Evans, *The Verbally Abusive Relationship*, helped Sandy understand what was happening to her. It taught her that verbal abuse is only the beginning. In this book, Evans explains the direct correlation between emotional abuse and illness. In the years when she was married to Tom, Sandy had been treated for the same disease over and over again. She could not overcome her symptoms. Finally, she leveled with her doctor and told him that she was in a toxic relationship. Her body knew what her mind could not accept. She had no idea what one person was capable of doing to another person's psyche and body. She learned things that she wished she hadn't had to learn.

Since her divorce, however, her nerves have calmed down and she is feeling well again.

Know Your Rights

For every case of domestic abuse that is reported, untold numbers of similar cases are just that—untold. There is no way of knowing the full extent of domestic abuse because of the countless women who suffer in silence. They don't know their rights, or they fail to demand that these rights be fulfilled.

The Victim's Bill of Rights is a model for treating all people with respect. This excerpt is adapted from *Victimology: An International Journal*.[47]

You have the right to...

- be safe and not be abused.

- change the situation.

- have freedom from fear or abuse.

- request and expect assistance from police and social agencies.

- share your feelings and not be isolated from others.

- desire a better role model of communication for yourself and for your children.

- be respected and be treated like an adult.

- leave the abusive environment.

- have privacy.

- express thoughts and feelings.

---

[47] *Victimology: An International Journal* 2, no. 3–4 (1977–1978): 550.

- develop individual talents and abilities.

- legally prosecute the abuser.

- make mistakes and be imperfect.

Margaret's Story

"He threw the cordless phone onto the concrete driveway—I watched as it was smashed to pieces. I felt terrified again when I saw that crazy look in his eyes. I knew then that he'd never change. At that moment, something clicked inside of me, and I thought, *He's never going to terrify me again*. I didn't know why, but this time I knew that I'd never go back. I was afraid for my mind and my body. I felt out of control."

Margaret wasn't the only one who knew that she had to get out of her marriage. She continued, "My son pleaded with me, 'Mom, how do you stand it? You have to get away from Daddy!' Here was my twelve-year-old son, giving *me* permission to leave. Somehow, that was all I needed to take the final step."

Margaret left everything familiar and moved to another state. Some people told her that her reaction was extreme, but it was a reaction that saved her life. And she's not alone. "Since then, I've heard amazing stories from other women who have also had to make drastic life changes. I try to encourage them. A seventy-year-old woman recently told me that she had been verbally abused by her husband for most of their marriage. She was afraid that his verbal abuse would escalate into physical violence, and it did. Fortunately for her, he died of cancer before he had the chance to kill her."

When this woman was in her late seventies, she remarried. Margaret said that she will always remember their conversations. "She was an inspiration to me," she said.

Diane's Story

For New York society, Diane had married very well—at least she thought she had. Early in their marriage, her husband Vernon's verbal abuse was sporadic. If he had had a good day at work, he would be in a good mood. But after a bad day, watch out! His verbal attacks on her character were so persuasive that she often believed him, or at least doubted herself. Was she really too sensitive, as he suggested? Did he have the right to blow up at every little incident? Over time, her sense of identity crumbled. He was eroding her spirit.

Meanwhile, Vernon's extravagant spending habits had racked up enormous amounts of debt, for which Diane was doling out big bucks to pay off. She wondered why she went along with the lies he told to the creditors. She couldn't seem to separate her identity from his anymore.

Diane took her marriage vows seriously—for her, divorce was not an option. Determined to fix things, she begged Vernon to seek help for the strain he was putting on their marriage. She implored him to go to a counselor, a doctor, or a minister, thinking that one of these individuals would surely provide a solution to their problems. Vernon eventually saw a doctor who evaluated him and then told Diane that her husband was mentally ill. Now, more than ever, Diane wondered how she could even think of leaving Vernon. After all, she had vowed to be his wife "for better, for worse…in sickness and in health." She was certain that her friends would be disappointed in her for leaving a sick man. But Vernon did not reciprocate his wife's commitment and devotion. He was sarcastic, and he mocked and denigrated her in every conceivable way. Diane still determined to stay with him. Yet, not long thereafter, a particularly harsh name-calling spree caused Diane to say, "Enough!" She finally mustered the courage to leave him, and she has never regretted doing so.

Jody's Story

Jody was in a situation similar to Diane's. When her husband, Tim, kicked a foot through the French doors of their dream home, she realized that she could have easily received the same treatment. Tim had already smashed several items around the house in his fits of rage. Time and again, Jody found herself inventing stories to tell friends and family members when they asked about the household repairs that followed Tim's destructive spurts. She felt ashamed—and guilty—each time she fabricated another story. Her dream home had become her prison, and instead of enjoying it, she wanted to escape. The day following the incident with the French doors, Jody went to a women's shelter while Tim was at work. There, she met many other women who were suffering in similar ways at the hands of their men.

After a few days at the shelter, Jody began to miss Tim. She tried to replay in her mind his abuse, namely, the times he had slapped her, and she realized that it would probably get worse. The stories of the other women in the shelter attested to this very fact. Fortunately for Jody, she decided not to risk going home to him, and she filed for divorce.

Tim did not fight the divorce and soon remarried. Not long afterward, his new wife called Jody to ask whether Tim had ever accused her of things that had never happened. Jody not only confirmed this experience, but she also filled her in on the abuses that had characterized her three-year marriage to Tim. His new wife thanked Jody and decided to get out of the marriage while it was still young. Within weeks, Tim was in divorce court for a second time.

Establish a Support System

After a traumatic breakup, it is important for you to nurture your broken spirit and restore its former vitality. It is normal to struggle with trusting other people after suffering the wounds and debasement of an untrustworthy abuser. Seek the support of family members, friends, and therapists or counselors to help you through the healing process. Isolating yourself from other people is the worst thing that you can do, even if you think doing so will protect you from further hurts caused by others. Interaction is necessary, and you will find the love

> ✍
> After a traumatic breakup, it is important for you to nurture your broken spirit and restore its former vitality.

and support of others to be as a soothing salve to your emotional wounds.

Gary Silverman is a Nevada attorney who deals exclusively with divorce cases. His clients are usually highly educated. In his practice, he sees fewer cases of physical abuse than he does emotional and verbal abuse. Many lawyers find it most challenging to help clients with issues of emotional abuse. Often, clients who have suffered emotional abuse are easily intimidated and have a difficult time standing up for themselves. Silverman said that he has observed a recurring pattern among his female clients: "A woman will call for an appointment to file for divorce. Just before the appointment, she will call and say that something has come up and she can't make it. Then, she will make another appointment. She calls again and says that she's decided not to go forward at all. Now, they've decided to go for couples' counseling."

Two or three years later, Silverman will hear from the same woman again. She will say that the counseling didn't work, and now she's feeling desperate; she wants a divorce. In the time that has elapsed, though, Silverman said that he will find nothing changed, except for maybe the woman's desperation. Now, she'll claim she's willing to "give away the ranch" and doesn't care about her financial settlement. She just wants out. Silverman continued, "As her attorney, I'll try to advise her of her rights. I'll also tell her about the long-term consequences of her decision to take less than she deserves. Some middle- and upper-class women will end up in poverty if their legal counsel does not protect them. When a woman is subjected to severe abuse, it's difficult for her to think rationally, so I try to do it for her."

Trying to increase awareness and solve abuse may be like trying to dig a man-made lake using only a spoon. But each spoonful gets us a little closer, and every little bit counts.

Mark Stets contracts with a domestic violence nonprofit organization in Las Vegas, Nevada. As a marriage and family counselor, he works with individuals who have perpetrated abuse and are undergoing court-ordered treatment. He leads participants through a twenty-six-week class, but "we have a very low success rate," Stets said. "It's their choice to come to the class or go to jail—and some prefer jail. Most come in with an attitude that says, 'Why isn't *she* here? *She's* the problem.' And I'd say that most of the men retain that attitude."

Stets said that his work is challenging, and even so, the vast majority of these men don't change. Many of them become repeat offenders—they end up abusing again. They may not repeat the same type or level of abuse that they had previously committed, but the abuse continues nonetheless, in some form or another. Stets said that he tells the abusers' partners to pay close attention to the "ex"-abusers' attitudes and behavior. If they exhibit no change whatsoever, their partners have no hope for a healthy relationship, and they should get out—the sooner the better.

Stets noted that counseling couples together about domestic abuse and related issues almost never works; moreover, it can be dangerous for the woman. If she is honest with the counselor and reveals her husband to be far from the Prince Charming she had originally perceived him to be, she may pay a hefty price later.

Abuse Affects—and Motivates—Even Those Who Are Not Victims

Abuse affects people from all walks of life, even those not directly suffering from it. Judy Abromowitz recalled a conversation about domestic violence in Israel that she overheard while she was serving as president of the Women's Division of the Jewish Federation of Greater Dayton, Ohio. From this conversation, she learned that the ugliness of abuse has no religious or geographical borders. Judy decided to become an advocate, and she helped form a partnership between the city of Dayton, Ohio, and the nation of Israel. Her committee reached out to rabbis and partnered with Artemis Center, Alternatives for Domestic Violence, and Womanline. Together, they promoted awareness of domestic violence by creating posters and "shoe cards," which are cards small enough to hide inside a shoe and which include telephone numbers and other important resources for victims. Today, there is an Interfaith Task Force committee at the Artemis Center, the work of which continues to save lives.

In 2001, Abromowitz was one of the women selected to receive the Ten Top Women of Miami Valley Award. When she was recognized thusly for her contributions to the fight to end domestic violence, she said that she was grateful to be making a difference, if only to save one life. Abromowitz didn't have to be a victim herself to see a need and to reach out to fill it. She just had to be a willing servant.

> ෨
>
> Margie saw emotional abuse every day in her home, but it was never discussed openly.

Margie's Story

Margie and her siblings lived with an alcoholic father and an emotionally absent mother who was so introverted that she had trouble talking to salespeople at a store. Margie saw emotional abuse every day in her home, but it was never discussed openly. It was as if there was an elephant in the kitchen, but everyone was complicit in pretending it wasn't there.

Margie's father kept a gun collection in the home. During one of his drinking sprees, he announced that he was going to kill Margie, her mother, and himself. Margie, who never enjoyed any physical contact with her father, ran to him and threw her arms around his waist, begging him not to shoot them. The begging worked, although the emotional abuse continued.

During another episode of inebriation, Margie's father was arrested, then taken to a mental institution, where he was treated for six months. When he came home, he told Margie's mother that he would never forgive her for putting him there. She left him once after he made this veiled threat but later returned. The accumulation of stress and fear caused her mother to have a series of three nervous breakdowns.

By the age of sixteen, Margie had endured all that she could take. She ran away from home, taking only her purse and the clothes on her back. Life was not easy for her, but she eventually met and married a kind man. Sadly, the painful memories of her childhood continue to haunt her. Margie is working on eliminating the trauma from her past.

Janet's Story

Janet knew that her marriage was disintegrating the day she and her husband moved from Kansas to Virginia, where he had accepted a job offer he just couldn't refuse. This day was also Janet's birthday, but her husband did nothing to acknowledge it. She hoped that a gentle reminder might prompt him at least to buy her a card, so when they stopped at a store on their way to Virginia, she drew her husband's attention to a rack of birthday cards. With disdain in his eyes, he threw a quarter on the floor and said, "Buy yourself a card."

Despite the tears rolling down Janet's face, he went on to say, "I'm tempted to just leave you here!" Having no money or means of traveling on her own, Janet sunk into the backseat of the car and tried to forget what had just happened. Every last iota of her personal dignity was gone, having been destroyed by her husband's verbal abuse.

Three years after the move to Virginia, Janet gave birth to the couple's third child. Her husband was not at the hospital during the delivery, and afterward, the hospital staff had to call him repeatedly to summon him to pick up his wife and new baby. Janet sat and waited for hours. Finally, she called her brother-in-law, who took her to her parents' home. She resolved never to return to her husband again.

Robert Fulghum, author of *All I Really Need to Know I Learned in Kindergarten,* told an insightful story that bears repeating.

In the Solomon Islands in the South Pacific, some villagers practice a unique form of logging. If a tree is too large to be felled with an ax, the natives cut it down by yelling at it. Woodsmen with special powers creep up on a tree just at dawn and suddenly scream at it at the top of their lungs. They continue this for thirty days. The tree dies and falls over. The theory is that the hollering kills the spirit of the tree. According to the villagers, it always works.

Ah, those poor naïve innocents. Such quaintly charming habits of the jungle. Screaming at trees, indeed. How primitive. Too bad they don't have the advantages of modern technology and the scientific mind.

Me, I yell at my wife. And yell at the telephone and the lawn mower. And yell at the TV and the newspaper and my children. I've even been known to shake my fist and yell at the sky at times.

Man next door yells at his car a lot. And this summer I heard him yell at a stepladder for most of an afternoon. We modern, urban, educated folks yell at traffic and umpires and bills and banks and machines—especially machines. Machines and relatives get most of the yelling.

Don't know what good it does. Machines and things just sit there. Even kicking doesn't always help. As for people, well, the Solomon Islanders may have a point. Yelling at living things does tend to kill the spirit in them. Sticks and stones may break our bones, but words will break our hearts….

Even an animal will cower when someone yells at it. Imagine how screaming at a child impacts the child and later the adult. If you have been the recipient of verbal abuse and uncontrolled anger, you already know how words can cut sharper than a sword. You don't have to continue taking it. You can make a decision to change your life before you, too, fall like a felled tree.[48]

---

[48] Robert Fulghum, *All I Really Need to Know I Learned in Kindergarten* (New York; Ballantine Books [a division of Random House], 2003), 19–20.

7

"I Married Dr. Jekyll but Live with Mr. Hyde"

୭

The picture-perfect life is not always what it seems. Just look at O. J. Simpson and Scott Peterson. Many people refused to believe that these two men could have been capable of committing the crimes with which they were charged. The world is full of street angels and house devils. You may feel like you are living a lie when your partner or spouse is kind and affectionate in public, yet brutal and unsympathetic in private. No one but you knows what goes on behind closed doors. Sometimes, you may doubt your own sense of reality. He treats you so kindly one moment and then terrorizes you the next. How did he get to be that way? In almost every case of a Jekyll and Hyde personality, the abuser grew up in a home where this personality typified his father's treatment of his mother, making the future abuser feel entitled to treat women this way.

> ୭
> The abuser grew up in a home where this personality typified his father's treatment of his mother.

Tim and Barry's Story

Tim hired Barry, an interior decorator, to redecorate his office. Within a month, Tim had developed a homosexual attraction to Barry. Tim had a larger-than-life personality, and he showered Barry with generous gifts. They would dine at the finest restaurants and drink expensive wines. For the first three months of their relationship, Barry thought that he had met the perfect partner.

But small snags soon developed and an apparently flawless relationship began to unravel. Tim was habitually late coming home but wouldn't call Barry to inform him. When Barry gently brought up the subject, requesting mere common courtesy, Tim grew annoyed and told Barry that he didn't appreciate his criticism. His anger grew, and he proceeded to erupt over this issue. This sequence happened time and again—one minute, Tim was utterly charming, and the next minute, he was terrorizing Barry. He would embarrass and humiliate him both in public and in private.

In spite of Tim's mercurial moods and volatile behavior, Barry stayed with him. The first five years had ups and downs, but Tim's charm and generosity kept Barry hanging on with hope. He was still irritated by Tim's chronic lateness, so, one night, he mentioned it again to Tim. Tim grabbed Barry and shoved him up against the wall. For the first time, Tim's verbal abuse had crossed the line and turned into physical abuse. He used such force that Barry's teeth were knocked loose, his nose was broken, and one of his eyes was bloodied. When Barry arrived at the emergency room, the social worker on staff looked him straight in the eye and said, "We both know that your injuries were no accident!" But Barry wasn't about to tell anyone what had really happened. In collusion with Tim, he told the hospital staff that the two had been drinking too much. Tim blamed the alcohol, but he also blamed Barry, saying that it was his fault for making Tim so angry that he was driven to drink. He told Barry that he couldn't take his constant nagging. By this time, Barry's thinking had become distorted and confused. He needed to learn that there is no excuse for abuse, not even when someone is roused to extreme anger.

Fortunately for Barry, a business transfer helped him to separate from Tim, at least emotionally. Tim pursued Barry for another year, pleading continually for another chance. He told Barry that he wanted to prove that he was different now. Tim finally wore him down, and Barry agreed to take Tim back with the caveat that if Tim ever raised a hand to him again, they would be done. Barry told Tim that if he ever hurt him again, there would be no discussion or argument; he would simply be gone.

A peaceable honeymoon period ensued, lasting three years. Then came the night that the relationship ended for good. Tim and Barry were in the car en route to a black-tie opera ball. They were in the midst of casual conversation when Barry said something that set Tim off. They reached a stoplight, and Tim turned from the steering wheel to raise his fist at Barry. No sooner had he clenched his fist than Barry opened the door and got out of the car. Tim pleaded with him to get back in the car, but Barry refused, reminding Tim about the conditions they had discussed three years earlier. Barry walked away from this eleven-year saga and never looked back. This decision may have saved his life.

One reason why Barry stayed with Tim so long is that Tim made repeated promises to stop his terrorizing behavior. Barry wanted to believe Tim's promises, and he always gave him another chance to fulfill them. Some victims remain with their abusive partners because these partners have threatened to kill them if they leave. They may find it easier to stay in abusive relationships than to leave them and face possible death. Many victims stay because they fear that no one will believe their stories.

Eileen's Story

Eileen suffered a mother's neglect and a father's alcoholism. She was the oldest of six children who had been fathered by three different men. After Eileen's parents divorced, her mother remarried a man who had several daughters. At first, this man treated Eileen with apparent kindness. He gave her coloring books, children's music recordings, and games. Soon, he started taking Eileen into the shower with him. He was a classic pedophile.

Violence followed. When Eileen was ten years old, she opened up to a friend, who then told her parents what Eileen's stepfather was doing to her. The report made its way to Eileen's school. When the school staff alerted Eileen's mother, she told Eileen to lie to the authorities and say that she had made up her story. She added that if Eileen didn't lie, she would be placed in a juvenile home. Fearing that the juvenile home would be even worse than her own home, Eileen denied her stepfather's abuse.

She was sent to a psychologist, but the sessions were fruitless—she refused to speak. By her early teenage years, she had learned to trust no one.

When the school year came to an end after Eileen's sophomore year, her parents locked her in her bedroom—for the entire summer. They gave her a potty-chair to use and brought each meal to her door. She felt imprisoned, as indeed she was, but she took some small comfort in the fact that her stepfather was no longer molesting her. What Eileen didn't know was that he had moved on to her younger sisters.

Eileen was released from her room when summer ended and school resumed. Now a junior in high school, she had stopped communicating altogether. Her sisters still confided in her, though, and they told her about their stepfather's abuse. This abhorrent news compelled Eileen to go to her mother again, this time about her sisters. Her mother finally sobbed, "I guess I always knew you were telling the truth." Eileen came to the terrible realization that her mother had known what was happening all along. Having felt that she had nowhere to go and no resources to survive on without Eileen's stepfather, she had essentially traded her children's well-being for a roof over her head. Eileen's mother finally divorced her stepfather, who then committed suicide. Eileen was eighteen. More than thirty years have passed, and Eileen is now a successful real estate broker. She has worked hard to overcome the abuse she suffered, as well as to forgive her mother and stepfather. But, says Eileen, forgiveness is not the same as acceptance of an abuser's behavior. For the sake of maintaining peace of mind, Eileen has cut off contact with the rest of her family. To see or speak with any of them conjures memories too painful to bear.

Be Wary of Charm

Keep in mind that the abuser is often a charmer. He may be quite likeable and fun, and these aspects of his personality trap you and keep you under his control, even when they are replaced with animosity and cruelty. You may be the only person who experiences his abusive side, and you will be hesitant to tell anybody for fear that they won't believe you. After all, he's so charming—why would they believe you? You may also feel ashamed and embarrassed. He is Dr. Jekyll with everybody else—kind, outgoing, charismatic. But with you, and you alone, he is Mr. Hyde—Dr. Jekyll's evil alter ego.

The Expenses of Abusive Alter Egos

Domestic violence is a significant health-care issue with major related costs. Every year, hospital emergency rooms in the U.S. treat more than 200,000 victims of domestic violence.[49] This number is not representative of the total cases, though, because four out of five victims won't go to the hospital. Only one in five victims ever seeks professional medical help. The American Medical Association estimates that nearly four million females every year are abused by their partners, and that every day, four women are murdered. Medical personnel are discovering that abused women have higher incidences of bowel disease, arthritis, and depression than the average female population.

The Canadian Institute of Health Research funded a $1.3 million research project to study the effects of abuse on the body. The three-year study also examined the response of women to Canada's justice system. The study was led by Dr. Colleen Varcoe, a nursing professor at the University of Victoria. Varcoe said that she is astounded by the number of health issues connected to abuse. Her research

---

[49] Bureau of Justice Statistics.

determined that abused women are not listened to and therefore fail to receive the assistance they require. In addition, it determined that the justice system is intimidating to many women, who largely misunderstand its processes and their options. "Now that we've completed the study, we want to use the results to educate service providers and policy makers about the importance of listening to women," Varcoe said, adding that "we also want them to involve women users of anti-violence systems in the creation and evaluation of services."

Incredibly, nearly one-third of all police time in the U.S. is spent on domestic violence-related disturbances.[50] Victims of domestic violence require medical care eight times more often than people who have never been abused.[51] Women will frequently make up stories instead of telling the truth about the nature of their injuries. If a woman seems mentally strung out, she'll say that she's just tired. It's difficult for her to feel that she is "telling on" her abuser. This situation is even more prevalent if both partners see the same physician, which makes uncovering the Mr. Hyde behind Dr. Jekyll extremely difficult.

The victims of intimate partner violence are more likely to seek medical assistance,[52] and this additional cost amounts to an estimated $4 billion annually.[53] And, as immense as this figure is, it represents only about 20 percent of what the total problem would cost if medical charges were applied to the abuse that goes unreported.

In December 2004, *People* magazine featured an article called "Woman without a Face," which told the story of Carolyn Thomas, a

---

[50] National Center on Women and Family Law, *Battered Women: The Facts*, 1996.

[51] Catherine L. Wisner, Todd P. Gilmer, L. Linda E. Saltzman, and Therese M. Zink, "Intimate partner violence against women: do victims cost health plans more?" *Journal of Family Practice* 48 [Issue 6] (1999).

[52] Frederick P. Rivara, Melissa L. Anderson, Paul Fishman, Amy E. Bonomi, Robert J. Reid, David Carrell, and Robert S. Thompson, "Healthcare Utilization and Costs for Women with a History of Intimate Partner Violence," *American Journal of Preventive Medicine* 32 [Issue 2] (February 2007): 89–96.

[53] *Costs of Intimate Partner Violence against Women in the United States, 2003.* Centers for Disease Control and Prevention, National Centers for Injury Prevention and Control. Atlanta, GA.

woman who was nearly killed by a gunshot wound from her abusive boyfriend just after he killed her mother. Reader Danny C. Newsome of Lucama, North Carolina, submitted the following response letter, which appeared in the January 2005 issue of the magazine:

> Carolyn Thomas is a victim of her own actions. As a police chief for twenty-nine years, I have seen battered women put themselves, family members and law enforcement in danger as they seek temporary help or shelter, only to return to their abuser. I feel Ms. Thomas can best help other abused women by telling them to reach out for permanent help and solutions from others and not return to hopeless and sometimes deadly relationships.

Mr. Newsome's advice is timely and imperative for any abuse victim. Carolyn Thomas now has her own foundation, Voices 4 All, that aims to improve the lives of domestic violence victims and increase their independence following recovery. To learn more about the Carolyn Thomas Foundation, visit www.carolyn-thomas.com.

If you have an abusive spouse who is a community leader or a pillar in town, you are caught in one of the trickiest traps. Other women may envy your marriage and consider you to be the luckiest woman in the world. Your husband may have been the recipient of a prestigious award, such as "Man of the Year," and you may be known as the woman who is married to the man who would give anyone the shirt off his back—except that he wouldn't give it to you. As he continues to chip away at your spirit, you completely lose your sense of "self." Your friends and colleagues may begin to think of you as a clingy, dependent woman. Before you drown completely, you need to find the strength to get out.

Patty's Story

Patty married the man every woman wanted. He came from a large, wealthy, well-educated family, and Patty thought that she had done well for herself in scoring such a catch. Little did she know that she had married a classic abuser, whose perpetrations extended to punching her in the face, beating her with a handgun, kidnapping her two young sons, and later raping her while they watched. After a few years, Patty and her children fled to a shelter in Sumter, South Carolina. Patty eventually experienced a transformational healing, which prompted her to assume the role of advocate for other abused women. She kept copious notes about her situation and the women whom she helped, believing that, one day, she would be strong enough to share her story.

Because Patty's husband was from a family of influence, he could always find a way to locate her. He had unlimited access to their children, even though he was a known abuser. After Patty left the shelter where she had sought refuge, she found an apartment and started her own house-cleaning business. This decisive step caused Patty's husband to realize that she was serious about leaving him for good. The prospect of losing Patty made him feel as if a part of himself was being ripped away, and he began stalking her to shorten the distance between them.

Driven to desperation, he threatened to kill Patty and the children. This he said over the phone—but with the full knowledge of the police, who had tapped his line. Due to his prominence and influence in the community, the divorce proceedings were unusually laborious. Fifteen court appearances and one thirteen-page decree later, the divorce was final. Patty now lives in another state, where she is an advocate for other women like her. She helped put teeth into South Carolina's stalking laws. She sought help from the YWCA and United Way. She was also commended by these agencies, as well as by Rep. John Spratt (D-SC), for her advocacy efforts. She is proof that one woman *can* make a difference!

One Woman Who Is Still Making a Difference

Jackie Kallen is the noted female boxing manager whose life was portrayed by Meg Ryan in the 2004 movie *Against the Ropes*. "Battered women come in all shapes, ages, backgrounds, and financial circumstances," Kallen said. "There are hundreds of thousands of women who are daily abused by the men in their lives. This situation must be stopped by getting to the root of the problem. The abusers need to be identified and prosecuted. Women must break their silence and come together as a group to end this age-old dilemma."

She went on, "We must realize the intense importance of getting away from the relationship and not returning. Too many women go back to their abusers because they feel they have nowhere else to go. That is untrue. There are people who care and organizations that are there to back up these women. It takes courage to leave and strength to stay away. But the reward is freedom—freedom from oppression, emotional and physical harm. Ultimately, your peace of mind will return."

> It takes courage to leave and strength to stay away.

She concluded with these assuring words: "No woman is alone in this battle. There are millions of other women ready to support and back you up. We must all come together to fight this war against domestic violence." With a clever allusion to the sport of boxing, Kallen added emphatically, "We must knock out domestic violence."

As you think about what you've read in this chapter, you need to face and accept the truth about your partner. If he has a Jekyll and Hyde personality, you need to stop hiding from the truth and realize that the dark Mr. Hyde will always be lurking behind even the friendliest Dr. Jekyll. The longer you deceive yourself into thinking Dr. Jekyll will prevail, the worse it will be for you.

Part II

GETTING OUT AND STAYING OUT
A STEP-BY-STEP GUIDE

8
THE IMPORTANCE OF A STRATEGIC ESCAPE PLAN

⪼

W hen a woman decides to leave an abusive relationship, how does she go about it? Where will she stay? How much money should she take along? Which important documents must she keep with her? This chapter provides a step-by-step procedure to follow when leaving an abuser. It explains how to develop a detailed escape plan that, once established, will make her ready to leave at any time. There are many dangers associated with the act of leaving an abusive partner or spouse, so this chapter will address specific safety precautions to keep in mind.

The following Personalized Safety Plan was contributed by the Office of the City Attorney, City of San Diego, California, and Barbara Hart and Jane Stuehling, Pennsylvania Coalition against Domestic Violence (PCADV), Reading, Pennsylvania.

Personalized Safety Plan

The following steps represent my plan for increasing my safety and preparing in advance for the possibility of further violence. Although I do not have control over my partner's violence, I do have a choice about how to respond to him/her and how to best get myself and my children to safety.

Safety during a Violent Incident

I can use some or all of the following strategies

If I decide to leave, I will _____. (Practice how to get out safely. What doors, windows, elevators, stairwells, or fire escapes would you use?)

I can keep my purse and car keys ready and put them _____ in order to leave quickly.

I can tell _____ about violence and request that they call the police if they hear suspicious noises coming from my house.

I can teach my children how to dial 9-1-1 for help.

I will use _____ as my code word with my children or my friends so they can call for help.

If I have to leave my home, I will go to _____. (Decide this, even if you don't think there will be a "next time.") If I cannot go to the location above, then I can go to _____ or _____.

I can also teach some of these strategies to some/all of my children.

When I expect that my partner and I are going to have an argument, I will try to move to a space that is low risk, such as _____. (Try to avoid arguments in the bathroom, garage, kitchen, near weapons, or in rooms without access to an outside door.)

I will use my judgment and intuition. If the situation is very serious, I can give my partner what he or she wants to calm him or her down. I have to protect myself until I/we are out of danger.

Safety When Preparing to Leave

Leaving the residence must be done with a careful plan in order to maximize safety. Batterers usually strike back when they believe that a partner is leaving the relationship. Always take your children with you, as safety permits.

I can use some or all of the following strategies:

I will leave money and an extra set of keys with _____ so I can leave quickly.

I will keep copies of important documents or keys at _____.

I will open a savings account by _____ (date) to increase my independence.

Other things I can do to increase my independence include: _____.

The local domestic violence program's hotline number is _____. The statewide number is _____. I can seek shelter by calling one of these numbers.

I can keep change for phone calls on me at all times. I understand that if I use my cell phone, the following month's telephone bill will tell my batterer those numbers that I called after I left. I need to be careful if I use my cell phone.

I will check with _____ and _____ to see who would be able to let me stay with them or lend me money.

I can leave extra clothes with _____.

I will sit down and review my safety plan as frequently as _____ in order to plan the safest way to leave the residence. _____ (domestic violence advocate or friend) has agreed to help me review this plan.

I will rehearse my escape plan and, as appropriate, practice it with my children.

Items to Take When Leaving

Items preceded by an asterisk on the following list are absolutely crucial to take along when you leave your abuser. If there is time, the other items might be taken or stored elsewhere outside the home.

These items might best be placed in one location so that they can be grabbed quickly.

When I leave, I should take:

*Identification for myself

Checkbook and/or ATM card

Credit cards

*Children's birth certificates

My birth certificate

Divorce papers

*Social Security cards

Medical records

School and vaccination records

*Medications

Address book

Keys (house, car, storage, etc.)

*Driver's license

*Green card

*Passport(s)

Work permit(s)

*Welfare identification

Safety with a Protection Order

The following are some steps that I can take to help the enforcement of my protection order:

I will keep my protection order in _____. (Always keep it on or near your person.)

I will give my protection order to the police departments in the community where I work, in those communities where I usually visit family or friends, and in the community where I live.

There should be a county registry of protection orders that any police department can call to confirm a protection order. I can check to make sure that my order is in the registry. The telephone number for the _____ County registry of protection orders is _____.

For further safety, if I visit other counties in _____ (state), I might file my protection order with the sheriffs in those counties.

I can call the Temporary Protection Order Office at _____ if I have a question or problem with my protection order.

I will inform my employer, _____, and my closest friend, _____, that I have a protection order in effect.

If my partner destroys my protection order, I can obtain another copy from the courthouse by going to the Clerk of Courts.

If my protection order is violated, I can call the police and report a violation, contact my attorney, return to the Temporary

Protection Order Office, and advise the court of the violation. I can also file a private criminal complaint with the law enforcement agency where the violation occurred.

If the police do not help, I can contact my advocate or attorney and can file a complaint with the police department itself.

Safety on the Job and in Public

Each battered person must decide if and when she will tell others that her partner has battered her and that she may be at continued risk. Each person should consider carefully which people to invite to help secure her safety.

I might do any or all of the following:

At work, I can inform my boss, the security supervisor, and _____ of my situation.

I can ask _____ to help screen my telephone calls at work.

When leaving work, I can _____ _____ .

If problems occur when I am driving home, I can _____ _____ .

If I use the public transit, I can _____ _____ .

I can use different grocery stores and shopping malls to conduct my business and shop at different hours.

I can use a different bank and take care of my banking at different hours.

I can also _____ .

Safety and Drug or Alcohol Use

The consequences of a battered partner's use of illegal drugs can be hard on her; it may harm her relationship with her children and put her at a disadvantage in legal actions with her battering partner. Therefore, the potential cost of the use of illegal drugs or alcohol should be carefully considered. Beyond this, the use of alcohol or other drugs can reduce a person's awareness and ability to act quickly to protect herself from her battering partner. Also, the use of alcohol or other drugs by the batterer may be used as an excuse for violent behavior. In the context of drug or alcohol use, a woman needs to make specific safety plans.

If illegal drug or alcohol use is a factor in my relationship with the battering partner, I can enhance my safety by doing some or all of the following:

> If I am going to use, I can do so in a safe place and with people who understand the risk of violence against me and are committed to my safety.
>
> I can also _____
> _____ .
>
> If my partner is using, I can _____
> _____ .
>
> To safeguard my children, I will _____
> _____ .

Safety and My Emotional Health

The experience of being battered and verbally degraded is physically exhausting and emotionally draining. The process of building a new life takes much courage and incredible energy. To conserve my emotional energy and resources in order to cope with hard emotional times, I can do some of the following:

> If I feel emotionally down and ready to return to a potentially abusive situation, I can _____ .
>
> If I have to communicate with the batterer in person or by telephone, I can _____ .

I can use "I can" statements with myself and be assertive with others.

I can tell myself "_____" whenever I feel others are trying to control or abuse me.

I can call _____, _____, and _____ when I need emotional support.

I can attend workshops and support groups at the domestic violence program, _____, or _____ to gain support and strengthen my relationships with other people.

Other things I can do to help me feel stronger are _____, _____, and _____.

Safety in My Own Residence

There are many things that a woman can do to increase her safety in her own residence. It may be impossible to do everything at once, but safety measures can be added one step at a time.

Safety measures I can use include:

I will change the locks on my doors and windows as soon as possible.

I will teach my children how to use the telephone and cell phone to call me and to call _____ (friend or other contact person) in the event that my partner takes the children.

I will tell those who take care of my children which persons have permission to pick up my children and that my partner is not permitted to do so. The people I will inform about pick-up permission include _____ (school), _____ (day-care staff), _____ (babysitter), _____ (teacher), and _____ (others).

I   will   inform _____ (neighbor)   and
_____ (friend) that my partner no longer resides
with me and that they should call the police if they observe
him near my residence.

If finances permit, I will install security systems, including additional locks, window bars, poles to wedge against doors, outside lighting, and other measures to protect me and my children.

Face the Facts and Commit to Finding Freedom

In order to survive emotional and physical abuse, you need to be honest with yourself regarding the reality of your situation. No matter how difficult it becomes, you will need to commit to a plan of action. You probably know that you need to make a change and that you must establish firm limits and boundaries. Most important, trust your instincts and have faith in yourself. Believe that you can accomplish your goal and do not minimize the severity of your situation, either to yourself or to others. Have the courage to follow through, even though this may be the most difficult life change you will ever make. Remember to listen to your inner voice, which always tells the truth.

9

THE SEVEN SECRETS OF STAYING OUT

෪

T he research that enabled me to write this book was provided by readers, my university students, abuse counselors, health and research professionals, and audiences around the world. I am grateful for your contributions. From your heartfelt stories and wise counsel, I have filtered several surefire keys to successfully staying out of an abusive relationship once you have escaped.

You are about to read the stories of Ann, Margaret, Teri, Vicky, and Maggie—five women who confirm the fact that domestic violence can happen to anyone, as well as an even more crucial fact: there *is* a way out. Not all of them discovered the way out, but each story conveys an essential secret that other women can use to make a successful getaway.

The Seven Secrets of Staying Out are:

1. Get real; destroy the illusion.

2. Cut off contact.

3. Create a financial action plan.

4. Put the children first.

5. Love yourself.

6. Toughen up for the long haul.

7. Focus on hope and healing.

Ann's Story

> ஐ
>
> Ann's husband told her that she would be "nothing" without him.

Ann was an eighteen-year-old college freshman when she began what would become an abusive relationship with a twenty-nine-year-old man. She married him just after graduating from college. More than fifteen years later, Ann described her husband as "controlling" and "manipulative." The abuse was most often verbal and mental, she said. Ann's husband told her that she would be "nothing" without him, and that she was incapable of making decisions and doing anything by herself. He tried to isolate Ann from her family, friends, and activities, threatening that if she didn't "behave," he would take the children away. This prospect terrified Ann, who would do anything to make her husband happy. She attended Al-Anon meetings to figure out how she could better support her abusive husband, who was an alcoholic. She even went to church and asked for prayer.

Ann stayed with her husband because she thought that it was the right thing to do for her children's sake. She did leave home several times, but she always went back; her husband would "smother" her with love by purchasing expensive gifts and apology cards. Ann's family wasn't helpful, either. Her mother wanted Ann to stay with her husband because he was a good provider. The children weren't happy, and when she finally ended the marriage, they expressed gladness and relief. When Ann finally realized that she could do nothing to make things better, she left, primarily at the impetus of escalating violence. She was forced to move into a shelter because her husband refused to leave the house.

When Ann left for good, she learned the **first secret**: *she had to get real and destroy the illusion*. Her husband appeared to be a happy family man to the eyes of outsiders. Ann described how her husband would sometimes apologize for what he had done in an effort to smooth everything over. His apparent remorse would take her in, over and over again. She was on an emotional roller coaster that peaked and dived with his mood swings. One day, he was upset by one thing; the next day, it was something else. Ann had started paying attention to the way her husband acted toward her, and she had stopped listening to his shallow words and false promises. Finally, she faced the facts. Her husband was abusing her, and he wasn't going to change. Faced with the reality of the situation, Ann had to engage in continual self-talk. She had to remind herself repeatedly that her husband was an abusive man. Today, she is free because she assimilated this truthful self-talk and stayed away from a man whom she knew to be abusive. She mastered the **first secret** of staying out: *get real; destroy the illusion.*

Margaret's Story

Margaret, now in her thirties, had completed high school and some college when she began her six-year marriage to a man who abused her. Domestic violence stains many of Margaret's memories, and she was told that she would be "nothing" without her partner. Margaret's husband would claim, for example, that the children were not his; he would tell the children, "Mommy is going to hell." One of their children even ran away from home to escape the emotionally depressive atmosphere. Margaret's husband did not want their house to look as if children lived there, so he was finicky about the games they played and messes they made. Leaving fingerprints on the glass coffee table constituted a huge crime, in his eyes.

Margaret felt like she was always walking on eggshells. She wanted to believe that everything would be okay, but she could feel her health deteriorating. As a newlywed, she had been healthy; now, she had a series of bowel and bladder problems. Her husband continued to tell her that she couldn't make it without him, and she began believing him. As a result of her husband's philandering, Margaret developed even more health problems. This vicious cycle continued until the day she woke up saying, "I have a chance for a life if I leave him. I have no chance if I stay." She repeated this mantra over and over again.

Margaret finally left the relationship. She returned three times, but only for the children's sake; the fourth time that she left, it was for good. She has never gone back, largely because she learned the **second secret**: *cut off contact*. Her husband was creative in coming up with ways to see her and talk with her after she had left. These times of contact would reconnect her emotionally, and she would start second-guessing her decision. She knew in her mind that the connection had to be broken, even if her heart said otherwise. She told herself that no matter what, she could no longer hear her husband's voice or be in his presence. The powerfully effective "no contact rule" broke Margaret's cycle through the revolving door of abuse. Today, she is able to see her ex-husband without feeling an urge to repair their broken bond. The second secret of staying out is, again, to *cut off contact* until you are able to see your ex-abuser without experiencing the desire to reunite.

> ॐ
> The powerfully effective "no contact rule" broke Margaret's cycle through the revolving door of abuse.

Teri's Story

Teri also experienced domestic violence as a child. She was a fourteen-year-old junior in high school when she and her nineteen-year-old boyfriend began a relationship that would last six years. The two eventually moved in together and had two beautiful children. But Teri's partner was abusive, and the home was filled with stress and tension. Teri described how each disagreement with her partner would end with *her* apologizing, regardless of who was at fault. When Teri tried to leave him, he trapped her financially—he hid the checkbook and credit cards. Cash was sparse, and Teri was financially dependent on her partner. She knew that she would face severe economic hardship if she chose to leave him. For a time, she put up with his abuse in exchange for financial security. Economic conditions today can afford a woman few viable options on her own, especially if she has a low education level and little professional experience. Many women get married and have children without developing marketable skills, and if their marriages fall apart, they are left with little hope of finding good, steady jobs. Government assistance to such women is often limited, and many of them dread welfare, preferring not to rely on it.

> ✎
>
> Many women get married and have children without developing marketable skills.

Teri began to save a little money each week. She opened her own bank account and arranged to have the statements mailed confidentially to a friend. She made copies of every important document she could find: her children's birth certificates, her car title, the insurance forms, Social Security cards, the deed to the house, mortgage papers, drivers' licenses, bank account numbers, savings passbooks, and credit cards/bank ATM cards. She was wise to *create a financial action plan*, the **third secret**. This plan helped her determine exactly how much money she needed to sustain herself and her children.

Teri's children were the ultimate impetus for her departure. She knew that it was unhealthy for her two young children to witness their father's rage. Still, Teri wasn't sure how she would make it on her own. She escaped to a shelter, where the staff and residents still talk about how she bought a car for ten dollars. The vehicle actually ran for an entire year. Teri now has a steady, well-paying job. She is a focused parent and a wise woman. The girl who dropped out of high school to set up house with her abuser has now completed her high school requirements and is enrolled in college. She learned the **third secret** of staying out: *create a financial action plan.*

The **fourth secret** is to *put the children first*. How does domestic violence affect children who are exposed to it? We discussed this topic in detail in chapter 3, but let's review some common characteristics of children from violent homes:

- They may not trust adults.

- They may experience anxiety attacks.

- They may have frequent nightmares and/or other sleep disturbances, such as bed-wetting.

- They may learn to be people pleasers and become especially preoccupied with pleasing the abusive parent.

- They may feel profound insecurity, which is manifested in low self-esteem and self-deprecating words or behavior.

- They may have stress-related physical illnesses early on in life.

- They may perform poorly in school, even if they are bright and intelligent.

- Worst of all, it is likely they will turn into abusers themselves.

Vicky's Story

By the time Vicky was twenty-eight, she and her abusive husband of nine years had had three sons. They were the reason she stayed in the relationship. Vicky had grown up in a family of strict religion, and although her family did not approve of the way her husband was treating her, they felt she had a responsibility to keep her family together.

One night, her husband's violence drove Vicky from her home. She and her three sons found themselves at a shelter. Battered and confused, Vicky used her time at the shelter to seek support and explore her options. She had had no schooling beyond high school, nor had she had any work experience, and thus no source of income. Her husband had not allowed her to pursue higher education or to have a career, thereby enforcing her dependency on him.

While she was staying at the shelter, Vicky struggled to make the right decision for herself and her children, but she eventually chose to return home with the children. Her parents commended her decision, calling it the responsible thing to do.

Vicky's husband continued to batter her. His beatings often left marks—but they were in places that no one else could see. He would also beat her skull and say, "I'm trying to pound some sense into you."

Vicky confided in her minister, who suggested she explore ways to make her husband happier. He explained that marriage can be stressful, but God rewards those who forgive others. He praised her for being a good wife and a fine mother by keeping her family together.

When Vicky started having severe headaches, she went to see the family doctor. She told him that her husband had beaten her repeatedly in the head. The doctor ignored this telling revelation and said that the headaches were due to stress. So, Vicky returned home to her husband. The headaches continued. She began questioning her decision to return home, but she believed that her husband was a good man who didn't really intend to hurt her or the kids. At the same time, she started praying that if anything should happen to her, the children would be able to stay with her parents. She clearly didn't trust her husband to provide a safe environment for their children in her absence, and yet she maintained belief in his goodness. She was a very confused woman.

Vicky's head pain became so severe that she had to be admitted to the hospital. That night, everyone thought that she would be okay. But Vicky knew then—as she had known all along—that there was no way out for her.

On her death certificate, it said that Vicky died of a cerebral hemorrhage.

Putting the children first does not mean allowing your abuser to kill you! Abuse is never okay, even in the name of keeping the family together. Children need a safe environment free of violence more than they need both parents. They need to be raised in an atmosphere of trust, where they are comfortable sharing their feelings. They need assurance that they are not alone, and they must also be taught to express their feelings without using violence. To learn this, children need to have role models who are not violent. Children from violent homes require contact with male authority figures who do not mistreat women in order to learn how to value and honor the women in their lives. These children also need to realize that they deserve to have their basic needs met. The **fourth secret** of staying out is to *put the children first* (but not at the expense of your own health or life).

As a woman frees herself from the abusive environment, she can take steps to enhance her self-esteem and thereby improve the quality of her life. The **fifth secret** is to *learn to love yourself.* You travel through life with one constant companion, and that is your "self." Don't let your closest companion become someone you don't even know!

This self-inventory can help you discover who you are. Please answer the following questions:

1. What do I like about myself?

2. What do I like best/least about myself?

3. How do I feel about my body?

4. How do I like to spend my leisure time?

5. What kinds of people do I prefer to be around?

6. What are the qualities I value most about other people?

7. What are the qualities I value least?

8. What kind of work do I find the most fulfilling?

When a woman has a healthy sense of self-esteem, she takes care of herself and does not ignore her own needs. She listens to wisdom and trusts her intuition. She is true to herself, even if it means losing the approval of others. She refuses to let negative people and unfortunate events determine the direction of her life. When she realizes that her abuser is controlling her, she will probably need time to grieve his lack of true love. Abuse and control have nothing to do with love, but accepting this fact can be difficult. Eventually, however, she will recover and come to know that she is worthy of true love and respect.

Even after she has achieved financial independence and put the children first by staying away from her abuser, there will still be times when she misses the good moments and memories spent with him, rare though they probably were. Often, this feeling is only temporary, but it is in these times that she must be particularly on her guard. She will require greater support than usual, too. It is much like the process of a recovering alcoholic. Even one drink may cause her to revert to old ways; one sip and she's back on the roller coaster of alcohol addiction. Many women mistakenly think that once they have left an abusive relationship, they can simply shut the door and start anew with ease. This is rarely the case, if ever. The **sixth secret** of staying out is to learn how to ***toughen up for the long haul***. Many individuals and organizations are ready to help women do just this.

Maggie's Story

Maggie lived in a beautiful, historic home in Indiana. She knew she needed to leave behind the memories these surroundings kept alive, but she felt stuck. She was emotionally drained from the abuse she had suffered, and she could not imagine packing up the contents of a 4,000-square-foot home and moving. A friend who lived on the East Coast offered her a couple of rooms in her home if she could break away. With her friend's encouragement, she woke up one morning and knew that it was time to go. Maggie sold her home and began a new life in another state. She downsized her belongings significantly, but she has never been happier—even though she faced a lot of challenges. She had to restart her career, make new friends, switch banks, and find a new doctor. She had difficulty explaining to friends why she had moved. Most people did not understand the reasons behind her seemingly dramatic decision to start over. But with her newfound freedom and the passing of time, many of her bitter memories have disappeared.

You have to be strong and courageous to move away from the familiar. Abuse may have begun to feel "normal," but you must know that domestic violence is not normal. You also have to make it everyone's business. Take advantage of the multitudes of national and local organizations that are reaching out to help. Whether you are a victim or simply a concerned individual, do not ignore the abuse and terror going on in your home and others'. Do something about it. Get involved. Speak out. To help or to get help, call the National Domestic Violence Hotline at 1-800-799-SAFE (7233). As individuals, groups, and organizations, we can make a difference. The **sixth secret** of staying out is to ***toughen up for the long haul***.

The **seventh secret** of staying out is to learn how to ***focus on hope and healing***. Two high-profile women who know all about the seventh secret are Oprah Winfrey and Christie Brinkley. In the January 2002 issue of *O* magazine, Oprah said that the biggest mistakes in her life have stemmed from her ceding power to someone else, believing that the love and approval of others were more important than the love that she had for herself. Many years ago, Oprah revealed that she had been in an abusive relationship. During this time, she believed that she needed a man to make her life all right. She soon realized that she was always trying to make him feel special, but no matter what she did or how hard she tried, it was never adequate to please him. She finally prayed for the strength to end their relationship. Oprah had come to realize the truth, which she professes to this day: she was all right just as she was. She was enough all by herself. It was only after this relationship ended that the world began to open up to her. If she had remained entangled in that relationship, she never would have performed in the 1985 film *The Color Purple*, a cinematic adaptation of the novel by Alice Walker, or launched her award-winning television show. That's hard to imagine!

Christie Brinkley is still haunted by terrible memories. In September 1999, she opened up in *Redbook* about her newfound joy—and lingering pain. She had married a man who mentally abused her, and her marriage was the only time in her life during which she was isolated from her parents. She found herself in the familiar trap of trying to see the "good" part of her husband. Finally, she couldn't take it anymore. She left when she was seven months pregnant. She said that everything in her was screaming to get out of the relationship, but she felt paralyzed and embarrassed. Then, she said to herself, *If you realize in your heart that something is not good for you and your family, throw away any thoughts about what anybody else might be thinking.*

Much has changed for Christie since those terrifying days. She found support and solace from a woman who helped her to understand what domestic violence is all about. She has often wondered what would have happened if she had not made the difficult decision to ignore others' opinions and leave the abusive relationship.

Oprah, Christie, and many other women prove that there is life after abuse. Healing is a lifelong process—physically, mentally, emotionally, socially, and spiritually. See through the confusion by moving at your own pace—do not rush or be impatient. It is easy to understand how a woman who identifies herself primarily as a wife and mother might feel that her life is over when her marriage ends. Who is she now? She is still herself—only stronger. She may have to rediscover her true self and redefine her identity, but she does *not* require her children or, least of all, an abusive spouse, to define her and give her value as a person. Your successful recovery depends on developing trust, honesty, love, and respect for yourself. A crisis can force you to create a new life—one that responds to your deepest, most fundamental needs. A crisis helps you to reevaluate your life and make the changes that can lead to peace and contentment. As you recover, you need to understand that change does not happen until there is faith and belief. What you think about, you bring about. What we expect, believe, and picture, we usually get. *"As he* [a man] *thinks in his heart, so is he"* (Proverbs 23:7 NKJV). This can also be read, "As she thinks in her heart, so is she." Believe that whatever you desire is already yours. *"Therefore I say to you, whatever things you ask when you pray, believe that you receive them, and you will have them"* (Mark 11:24 NKJV).

Focus daily on the following affirmations:

- I can trust my own feelings and perceptions.

- I am not to blame for being abused.

- I am not the cause of another's irritation, anger, or rage.

- I deserve freedom from mental anguish.

- I can say no to what I do not like or want.

- I do not have to take the abuse.

- I am an important human being.

- I am a worthwhile person.

- I deserve to be treated with respect.

- I have power over my life.

- I can use my power to take good care of myself.

- I can decide for myself what is best for me.

- I can make changes in my life if I want to.

- I am not alone; I can ask others to help me.

- I am worth working for and changing for.

- I deserve to make my own life safe and happy.

- I can count on my own creativity and resourcefulness.

The **seventh secret** of staying out is to ***focus on hope and healing***.

Nobel laureate Anatole France spoke these wise words about the process of recovery: "All changes, even the most longed for, have their melancholy; for what we leave behind us is part of ourselves; we must die to one life before we can enter into another!"

Epilogue

Scott Jordan is a retired family court judge and faculty member of the National Judicial Institute on Domestic Violence. Judge Jordan's domestic violence work began in the early 1970s, when he and his family voluntarily sheltered battered women in their home. In an article entitled "Context Is Everything: Domestic Violence in the Real World," authors Billie Lee Dunford-Jackson, J.D., and Judge Jordan state that a failure to understand domestic violence is likely to have drastic consequences. Judges and attorneys involved in any case related to domestic violence must understand both the true nature of domestic violence and the dynamics of the individual case. They must create orders that ensure the safety of all family members and protect their rights.

Judge Jordan emphasizes that a victim of domestic violence is not alone and the abuse is not her fault. He says that the patterns of power and control are sadly all too pervasive in our society. Domestic violence has been illegal for more than thirty years. Specific laws differ from state to state, but before 1975, domestic violence was not considered a crime in the United States. Today, law enforcement officers, attorneys, and judges are becoming more and more educated about this issue now that it is not only illegal, but also increasing in incidence. Battered women have come together both locally and nationally, and there are now widespread resources available to help women and their children to find safety and the financial means to live independently.

Judge Jordan says that the real answer to the issue of domestic violence is a community-wide comprehensive response that would involve police, prosecutors, judges, parole and probation officers, treatment providers, schools, battered women's support networks, and the public. All of these individuals and entities must be on the same page and completely committed to ending any and all forms of abuse. Batterers need to get a clear and consistent message that abuse entails harsh consequences.

Already, many communities in the United States have come close to fulfilling the vision of Judge Jordan. Several communities have created a community-wide comprehensive response plan to deal with domestic violence. Much has been done in the past thirty years, but much remains to be done. And no effort is too small. You can make a difference.

Recommended Reading and Resources

Browne, Angela. *When Battered Women Kill*. New York, New York: The Free Press (Simon & Schuster), 1987.

Burlingame, Michael. *The Inner World of Abraham Lincoln*. Champaign, Illinois: The University of Illinois Press, 1994.

Carnes, Patrick J., Ph.D. *The Betrayal Bond: Breaking Free of Exploitive Relationships*. Deerfield Beach, Florida: Health Communications, Inc., 1997.

Cloud, Henry, and John Townsend. *Safe People: How to Find Relationships That Are Good for You and Avoid Those That Aren't*. Grand Rapids, Michigan: Zondervan, 1995.

Cook, Philip. *Abused Men: The Hidden Side of Domestic Violence*. Westport, Connecticut: Praeger Publishers (Greenwood Publishing Group, Inc.), 1997.

Davis, Jeanie Lerche. "Psychological Abuse = Physical Abuse." *WebMD Health News*. October 24, 2002. http://www.webmd.com/mental-health/news/20021024/psychological-abuse-physical-abuse.

Ellis, Albert, Ph.D., and Marcia Grad Powers. *The Secret of Overcoming Verbal Abuse: Getting Off the Emotional Roller Coaster and Regaining Control of Your Life*. Hollywood, California: Wilshire Book Company, 2000.

Engel, Beverly. *The Emotionally Abusive Relationship: How to Stop Being Abused and How to Stop Abusing*. Hoboken, New Jersey: John Wiley & Sons, 2002.

Evans, Patricia. *Controlling People: How to Recognize, Understand, and Deal with People Who Try to Control You*. Avon, Massachusetts: Adams Media Corporation, 2002.

———. *The Verbally Abusive Relationship: How to Recognize It and How to Respond*. Avon, Massachusetts: Adams Media Corporation, 1996.

Fulghum, Robert. *All I Really Need to Know I Learned in Kindergarten.* New York, New York: Ballantine Books (Random House), 1986, 1988, 2003.

Heitler, Susan. *The Power of Two: Secrets of a Strong and Loving Marriage.* Oakland, California: New Harbinger Publications, Inc., 1997.

Jakes, T. D. *Woman, Thou Art Loosed!: Healing the Wounds of the Past.* Shippensburg, Pennsylvania: Destiny Image Publishers, 1993, 2001.

Katherine, Anne, M.A. *Boundaries—Where You End and I Begin: How to Recognize and Set Healthy Boundaries.* New York, New York: Parkside Publishing Corporation, 1991.

———. *Where to Draw the Line: How to Set Healthy Boundaries Every Day.* New York, New York: Fireside (Simon & Schuster, Inc.), 2000.

Lerner, Harriet. *The Dance of Anger: A Woman's Guide to Changing the Patterns of Intimate Relationships.* New York, New York: HarperCollins, 1985, 1997.

Liardon, Roberts. *Breaking Controlling Powers.* New Kensington, Pennsylvania: Whitaker House, 2000.

Miller, Dusty. *Your Surviving Spirit: A Spiritual Workbook for Coping with Trauma.* Oakland, California: New Harbinger Publications, Inc., 2003.

Stern, Robin. *The Gaslight Effect: How to Spot and Survive the Hidden Manipulation Others Use to Control Your Life.* New York, New York: Morgan Road Books, 2007.

Walker, Lenore. *The Battered Woman.* New York, New York: Harper & Row, 1979.

DOMESTIC VIOLENCE RESOURCES

National Domestic Violence Hotline: 1-800-799-SAFE
(1-800-787-3224 for the hearing impaired).

Face to Face—free plastic surgery for domestic violence victims.
Mary Lynn Moran, M.D., surgeon.
Donate at www.glamour.com. (A ten-dollar donation helps
pay for anesthesia, medications, and supplies.)

UNIFEM—The United Nations Development Fund for Women
Promotes antirape laws, labor rights, and ending domestic
violence around the world. For more information,
visit www.unifem.org/support.

About the Author

Jane Boucher received her bachelor of science and master of arts degrees from The Ohio State University. She has done doctoral work at the University of South Florida and has been an adjunct professor at the University of Dayton, Wright State University, Sinclair Community College, and Antioch University McGregor. She also served as Associate Director of the Antioch University McGregor Organizational Institute.

The author of seven books, she uses both the podium and the pen to promote personal and professional excellence. Her best seller, *How to Love the Job You Hate*, has been endorsed by Dr. Kenneth Blanchard, author of the best seller *The One Minute Manager*. She has been interviewed and profiled by *Forbes* and the *New York Times*. She is a nationally syndicated newspaper columnist and contributes to business journals across the country.

Jane worked with at-risk youth before launching her professional speaking career. As a Fortune 500 professional speaker, corporate trainer, Certified Mediator, and consultant, she tells it like it is to organizations and companies such as the United States Senate, the United States Department of Agriculture (USDA), the Department of the Navy, the United States Air Force, the Federal Deposit Insurance Corporation (FDIC), Merrill Lynch, General Motors, Toyota, the Medical Group Management Association (MGMA), IBM, NCR, the International Association of Hispanic Meeting Professionals (IAHMP), and Prudential of Europe. She has received praise from such notables as Sen. Orrin Hatch (R-UT) and has shared the platform with General Norman Schwarzkopf, Bernard Siegel, M.D., and Nevada Governor Kenny Guinn. Not shy with the media, she has been featured on more than one thousand radio and television programs, including those aired by CNBC, CBN, and CNN.

Jane is one of the most dynamic women on the speaking circuit today. The National Speakers Association awarded her the Certified Speaking Professional (CSP) designation, a distinction held by less than 8 percent of professional speakers.

She can be reached with feedback or to discuss speaking engagements at jane@janeboucher.com.

Authority Abusers (new and expanded)
George Bloomer

We would be living in a world of complete chaos if there were
no one in authority. Godly authority in homes, churches, and
relationships is meant to lead, protect, and preserve us. Authority
abuse, on the other hand, shatters lives, destroys marriages, and
does great harm to individuals. In this revealing book are the
keys to breaking free from the bondage of spiritual abuse. Bishop
George Bloomer shows how you can recognize authority abusers,
identify their controlling tactics, and restore the abused and the
abuser. You can break free from spiritual bondage and experience
God's deliverance!

ISBN: 978-1-60374-046-3 ✦ Hardcover ✦ 208 pages

WHITAKER
HOUSE

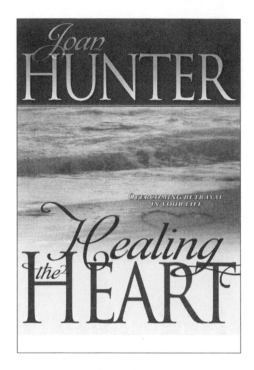

Healing the Heart
Joan Hunter

In this life-changing book, Joan Hunter shares her testimony of how she overcame rejection and the worst betrayal imaginable. No matter your circumstances, God wants to minister to you through Joan's insights and practical advice. You can find the strength to achieve when the world says you will fail, receive a new heart when yours has been broken by betrayal, and live a life of blessing, even after feeling like you have nothing left. Your broken heart can heal, and Joan's inspiring story will make this truth come alive for you.

ISBN: 978-0-88368-130-5 • Trade • 192 pages

WHITAKER
HOUSE

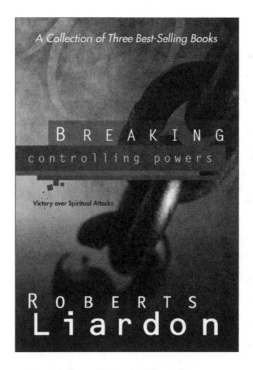

Breaking Controlling Powers
Roberts Liardon

Roberts Liardon has combined three of his best-selling books to give you the spiritual weaponry you need to fight the good fight of faith! This book will equip you to break free of manipulative relationships, learn to say no without feeling guilty, survive attacks on body, soul, and spirit, and receive the Holy Spirit's power. If controlling people are coming between you and God, or if you feel like the whole world is against you, then this three-in-one volume is for you.

ISBN: 978-0-88368-554-9 ♦ Trade ♦ 272 pages

WHITAKER
HOUSE

A Wife's Prayer
Pamela Hines

This book is a beautiful collection of scriptural prayers and true stories of hope and restoration. When a wife seeks the Lord's wisdom and intercedes on behalf of her husband, the marriage—and the family—benefits in many areas, including health, prosperity, protection, guidance, career, vocation, desires, affections, and many more. Pray and watch as God transforms your husband into your family's spiritual leader. By helping him become a mighty man of God, you will also reap family blessings for generations to come.

ISBN: 978-0-88368-204-3 ♦ Trade ♦ 176 pages

WHITAKER
HOUSE